TRAINING
THE
NEW SUPERVISOR

TRAINING
THE
NEW SUPERVISOR

James E. Gardner

a division of
AMERICAN MANAGEMENT ASSOCIATIONS

Library of Congress Cataloging in Publication Data

Gardner, James E
  Training the new supervisor.

  Bibliography: p.
  Includes index.
  1. Supervision of employees—Studying and teaching.
I. Title.
HF5549.15.G37   658.4'07'124   79-55060
ISBN 0-8144-5564-6

© 1980 AMACOM
A division of American Management Associations, New York.
All rights reserved. Printed in the United States of America.

FIRST PRINTING

To the kids:
Nancy, Ned,
John, and Mary

Preface

A S A CREATOR, conductor, and administrator of training programs for new supervisors for many years, I was somewhat
surprised (and a bit dismayed) to discover, when I sat in on a
session on supervisory training at the 1977 National Conference of
the American Society for Training and Development, that many
trainers did not quite know how to go about training supervisors
and were raising fundamental questions about content, approach,
schedule, and other topics. Of course, I recalled that I had been in a
similar quandary in the early years. But what struck me as especially
ironic was that such elementary questions were being asked at a
time when the inquirers had access, in the conference, to a dazzling
array of programs purporting to be good for the supervisor.

There are several issues here, I believe: specifically, whether
programs being offered to industrial trainers and operating managers realistically address needs or are inconsequential fluff;
whether they genuinely serve the interests of the client or are
ill-fitting encrustations serving the interest of the advocate primar-

ily; and—if all doubts are resolved as to utility and validity—whether they can be installed in an industrial organization in a meaningful and effective way.

The problem is compounded by the need for "translation" when programs are produced by unrelenting academicians (fortunately, there are other kinds), who tend to write primarily for each other in a jargon of their own. The necessity for translation exists also with research findings emanating from the social scientists and behavioral scientists.

What the training profession needs in greater number and the individual organization often desperately needs are gatekeepers and translators who, in addition to shooing away the obvious charlatans, can look critically at what is forthcoming at the sales counter and in the literature, determine what is truly useful and practical for the operating manager, and then bring it to manageable size and shape, so that it fits into the existing managerial framework.

The people who serve these functions have a thankless task. They run the risk of misinterpreting or simplifying or misapplying the work of the academics and researchers, or at least of missing some of the nuances and qualifications. They may dismiss good material or indications as unworthy or impossible to use. On the other hand, they risk alienating the operating managers by appearing too scholarly and by advocating "outlandish" approaches (anything beyond the tried and true—or at least the tried). So they may be damned as insufficiently academic by the academic and insufficiently practical by the practical. They may please no one.

But if they are thick-skinned enough and self-reinforced enough, and if they stand steadfast, they are our most hopeful means of uniting the contributing, though divergent, elements in the interest of effective training.

This is my own apologia. Through a good part of my occupational life I have tried to translate and apply research findings in industrial settings, to synthesize as best I could the experimental and experiential. I have attempted in this book to continue the effort.

I must make a few final comments about the book itself, in regard to possible sins of omission and commission. Many trainers and operating managers are troubled by problems encountered by hourly paid employees in adjusting to supervisory jobs. I have not dealt with this issue as a separate subject because I believe the simple answer is that these employees will adjust if they know how to supervise, if we have ensured, through adequate training, that they have developed the required supervisory skills. Giving them the needed skills is what this book is all about.

Finally, I am a firm advocate of placing and training qualified women in supervisory jobs, and I have done what I could to foster such movement in my own company. I hope, therefore, that women who read this book will be understanding and gracious enough to accept the traditional singular designation of "he" and "him" as applying to male and female alike. As a grammarian and admirer of the language, I would much dislike peppering the book with the awkward double designation.

JAMES E. GARDNER

Contents

TRAINING
THE
NEW SUPERVISOR

CHAPTER 1

What the New Supervisor Needs Training In

THE FIRST STEP in planning the training of new supervisors is to determine what the supervisor is expected to do. What is his job? Such information is necessary to make realistic decisions about what the supervisor needs training in and to develop strategies for giving the training.

In trying to define the job, it is not necessary to reinvent the wheel. It would be a poor company, indeed, that did not have a written job description of some sort or, tucked away in the minds of supervisors and superiors, a world of data that could be elicited and organized into a written statement—or the resources for making current observations of supervisory behavior. Even traditional data have uses, if we are willing to update them.

But the more fundamental issue, assuming the availability of valid data, is how to use them. This matter requires, first, the answers to a few simple questions: How much data do we settle for? How far do we take the analysis? How do we organize the data so as genuinely to identify training needs?

Inadequacy of Responsibility Statements

A short statement of so-called responsibilities will not serve. Obviously, supervisors do have responsibility for such global matters as output or efficiency of operations, quality of product, maintenance of employee safety and health, effective utilization of personnel, and development and maintenance of a competent workforce. But it is not the bald responsibilities that are the stuff of training. It is, instead, the means of meeting their responsibilities—the activities and their skillful execution—which new supervisors must master. Unless they are given specific training in what to do and how to do it, new supervisors have no recourse but to structure their own jobs, establishing activities and routines which, in their uninformed judgment, will represent an execution of their responsibilities. And in such case supervisors have no learning method to rely on but trial and error.

Even attaching performance goals and indexes to major responsibilities does not give us an adequate basis for identifying training needs. It is not difficult to find measurement indexes related to responsibilities. Their very ubiquity invites us to use them for all sorts of purposes. Most companies have plentiful records purporting to measure output, efficiency, quality, labor costs, supply costs, waste, accident incidence, accident costs, turnover, and absenteeism. And if the "scores" on such indexes are under the control of the supervisor or significantly influenced by him, his performance may be judged by them and goals set by them. But even valid indexes tell us only about the level of the supervisor's performance and nothing about how he is to achieve a satisfactory level. We simply do not train supervisors with primary reference to broad responsibilities and global indexes associated with them.

Sometimes we busy ourselves with statements concerning supervisory authority—the companion piece to responsibility—defining it in terms of either upward relationships (freedom from restraint imposed from above) or downward relationships (freedom to direct employees). With the former, we are at pains to specify the supervisor's degree of authority in various matters; we become very precise as we proceed through the academic exercise of drawing lines among the matters which a supervisor can (1) handle independently, (2) handle with information to his superior, (3) handle with prior information to his superior, (4) handle only with prior approval from his superior—and so on—along a scale from autonomy to total dependence.

Such definitions are uncertain grounds for determining training needs. Jobs are rarely carried out by adhering to such distinctions. It is natural for supervisors to progress from dependence to relative independence (within broad hierarchical bounds) as they advance in job competency—a development a wise superior will attempt to bring about in an organized and systematic way.

Nor does a general statement, accompanying the various responsibilities, of the supervisor's inherent power to direct employees and impose sanctions offer much assistance in identifying training needs. What is needed is a functional statement, related to activities, which outlines valid expressions of authority and limitations on authority imposed by company policy, union contract, and government regulations.

Translating Responsibilities into Functions

Thus it is useful to translate general statements of responsibilities into functions in order to get closer to a rational basis for surveying training needs. These functions represent, in a general way, what the supervisor must do to meet the responsibilities; in effect, they are the roles played by the supervisor in this effort. Functions include monitoring, reporting, investigating, assigning, training, and adjudicating. The roles are those of monitor, reporter, investigator, and so on.

Table 1 lists the major functions associated with supervisory responsibilities. The table is not intended to be rigid or complete; it is merely illustrative. There may be good argument for putting certain functions under a different responsibility heading or under a new heading altogether. And there may be more functions than those represented here. The main point is to compile a comprehensive list of what needs to be done to perform the supervisory job.

TABLE 1.
Supervisory responsibilities and related functions or roles.

Responsibility	Functions or Roles
Maintaining output and efficiency of production	Monitoring production in relation to schedule; investigating and correcting output difficulties Monitoring operation and condition of machinery; investigating and correcting maintenance problems Monitoring production costs; investigating and correcting above-standard costs
Maintaining quality of product	Monitoring condition of materials and quality of items produced or in process; investigating and correcting causes of substandard quality
Maintaining employee safety and health	Monitoring physical hazards, health hazards, and unsafe acts; correcting unsafe conditions and acts Reporting and investigating accidents; correcting causes of reported accidents Safeguarding of employees and property in security matters
Utilizing and compensating employees	Assigning work and making assignment changes Establishing and monitoring job methods Installing and monitoring pay standards Administering payroll
Developing personnel and stabilizing workforce	Training and retraining employees Monitoring employee performance; investigating and correcting causes of substandard performance Hiring, promoting, and transferring employees Hearing and adjudicating complaints and grievances Maintaining discipline

The currency of responsibilities is a pertinent issue. Rarely do general responsibilities become out of date. The supervisor is inevitably concerned with efficiency of operation, output and quality of products, and the utilization, development, stability, and protection of his workforce. These broad responsibilities do not change appreciably unless there are basic changes in the very nature of the enterprise or unless significant new legal or other requirements compel a reshaping. An example is the expansion of the protection of employees to include matters of health as well as injuries under recent state laws and the federal Occupational Safety and Health Act. When such rare changes in responsibilities do occur, we must ensure that they are translated into changes in function and activity.

In the normal course of events, functions too remain relatively stable. In most cases they have evolved historically as the organization gave shape to its various jobs and tested out the division of labor. In these functions are embedded the experience of earlier supervisors and the informed judgment of higher line management. Though not exclusively so, these functions largely involve monitoring—monitoring machine efficiency, product quality, and employee performance, and taking action when the monitoring uncovers a problem.

Specifying Activities

The next and most crucial step in specifying supervisory training needs is to reduce the functions to statements of activities. That is, we must define the specific procedures the supervisor must engage in—and engage in skillfully—to discharge the functions effectively. It would be foolish, indeed, to stop with functions and permit the new supervisor to devise his own activities for carrying them out. Instead, we should train him in the approved way or in the demonstrably effective way. Later, on the basis of experience, the supervisor may participate in revising formal procedures and will certainly exercise some control over his own informal pattern of activities.

These activities, as we define them, become the grist for our training mill; they are, in effect, the scripts for the various supervisory roles. We next decide what type of training is needed and when to teach the supervisor to perform the activities—with emphasis on how they are best done and on the development of skill in doing them. Training should not stop with specifying what is to be done; it is aimed at producing skill of execution. Some of these activities will involve relatively impersonal procedures, some will involve interpersonal exchanges, and some will require both. Some can be taught with a minimal training effort involving few approaches; others will require a long-range training strategy that uses a number of techniques.

For example, if the supervisor's activity in administering the company benefits program is limited to explaining the provisions of plans to employees—if he is not otherwise involved in carrying out the plan—our training need not go very far. But it should go far enough even in this restricted activity. We should not only teach the facts of our benefit plans to the supervisor (lectures will serve) but also make sure that he can transmit such information effectively. At the other extreme—in quality matters, for example—a supervisory activity may require knowledge, administrative skills, communication skills, and teaching skills. In such a case, our training will have to be much more extensive.

As we specify supervisory activities, it is useful to keep in mind the total cycle of training. Training begins with assessing what needs to be learned, using certain approaches to teach it, and keeping track of how the learning is progressing. In regard to activities—which should be the focus of concern in supervisory training—we ascertain and specify the activities that must be learned, teach them in a discriminating way, and measure their effectiveness.

Certain groundrules should guide us in these efforts. First, we should specify the learning needs in detail, but with a certain restraint. Sterile knowledge—knowledge that is not utilized in any activity, not even transmitted to someone, and is not a necessary background for activities—need not be specified or taught. This would seem to be an obvious rule; yet trainers seem to waste precious time developing pointless material. Second, as suggested earlier, not every activity will require the same training approaches or the same number of training interventions. Third, the most useful measurement tools in training are those intermediate or immediate indexes of how well the activities are being carried out. We will examine later, in some detail, the kinds of indexes which a genuine training effort requires. At this early stage, it is important to note only that some popular indexes will not serve our training purpose because they are too far removed from supervisory activities. These include global indexes attached to so-called responsibilities, "floating" indexes that cannot clearly be associated with activities, indexes not significantly influenced by what a supervisor does, and summary indexes that give long-interval outcomes.

In identifying and specifying training needs, we should bear in mind that a supervisor is involved in two kinds of activities: procedural and interpersonal. Procedural activities are based on formal or informal procedures, both technical and administrative. Interpersonal activities involve contacts with employees for exchanging information and other purposes. As we proceed to examine procedural and interpersonal activities, we should keep in mind the need to apply the same tests for currency to which responsibilities and functions are subjected.

PROCEDURAL ACTIVITIES

Formal procedures abound in industry. They are the product of the plant's or department's own ingenuity and insight, or a staff department project or study, or, more likely, of a joint effort of staff and line. Suppose, for example, that the supervisor has the function of monitoring the quality of product. Formal procedures may include inspecting the mechanical operation of machines at certain times (under a sampling arrangement, perhaps); using a checklist for such inspection; systematically examining the beginning raw materials, materials in process, and final product; reporting findings on a prepared form; and reviewing reinspection reports from the Quality Control Department.

Even if activities are not performed in accordance with a formal procedure, they can still be identified through observation of what successful supervisors do. Such observation can be the basis for a statement of activities to use in training new supervisors.

Procedural activities need to be reexamined periodically to determine whether they are still instrumental in discharging the function. It is common, for example, to find a supervisor performing traditional paperwork—such as preparing certain operational reports—which no longer serves a useful purpose.

Assuming that the procedural activities are effective means of carrying out the supervisor's function, it is not enough for us simply to make sure that he is aware of them and is performing them; we must also deal with "how well." There is a wide range of skill in checking out a machine, for example, no matter how fully we circumscribe the act with checklists and schedules. Training is concerned not only with the act but with its successful execution. In even minor activities, skill must be developed.

INTERPERSONAL ACTIVITIES

In interpersonal supervisory activities—that is, those involving an interchange with employees—the usual intent is to elicit information; to give information, directions, and orders; to instruct or correct; or to perform a combination of these. Such interactions (attached to various functions) account for a large percentage of the supervisor's time and include informing employees about safety hazards, disciplinary rules, quality standards, production expectations, work assignments, and pay rates; investigating the bases of complaints and grievances; giving instruction in job tasks; and explaining changes in job methods and procedures. When changes occur in any aspect of the employee's job or in surrounding conditions, the supervisor must inform the employee.

There are cautions to be observed in designating which interpersonal activities are to be learned. We should specify those activities which experience has shown to be effective in carrying out a function. They are not always easy to pin down and may require careful observation of successful supervisors. Although a model may thus be required, the objective is not to have the new supervisor slavishly copy a certain supervisory style. In training the new supervisor, we should not focus on someone else's unique manner of getting and giving information, for example, but instead should establish, in the new supervisor's pattern of activities, those techniques of communication which will work for any supervisor, such as organization of material, repetition, emphasis, playback, and other proven means of avoiding miscommunication.

At the beginning stages of a new supervisor's development, there is good reason to restrict his training in interpersonal matters to the primary purpose of helping him, as with procedural activities, to structure the job. The emphasis should be on the supervisor's use of information to clarify the role and status of employees and to assist them in carrying out their assigned tasks with skill and within the rules. This is not to advocate a neglect of relationships. But since the new supervisor cannot learn everything in quick order, the first item of business is to teach him to organize his job by bringing the technology and the administrative procedures and rules under control and by shaping a workforce that will be a source of relatively predictable output and outcomes related to operational objectives.

To achieve this end, the new supervisor will have to concentrate on two major determinants of job performance: training and job conditions. The supervisor can see to it that efficient job methods are used, can clarify job assignments if necessary, can ensure that performance standards and expected levels of output are understood, and can provide the training to help employees who lack skill to reach expected levels. He can also take steps, in conjunction with his monitoring functions, to make jobs more manageable if performance is suffering, eliminating bottlenecks in the flow of material as best he can, providing enough supplies and equipment, arranging for adequate maintenance of machinery, ensuring that the material is of workable quality, and improving whatever surrounding conditions are harmful to performance.

A more direct effort at motivation—a third major determinant of performance—can come later, when training and job conditions are under control and when the new supervisor has had adequate opportunity to know his employees. At that point he can more fruitfully turn his attention to the availability of rewards and the means of maximizing them.

The new supervisor should not become preoccupied with interpersonal activities for the purpose of endearing himself to employ-

ees or creating a warm and gratifying relationship with them right at
the start. Such a preoccupation may well interfere with the supervisor's early development of technical and administrative competency, which is essential in building a relationship of respect. The
point should be made that a salutary working relationship will depend on the employees' degree of confidence in the new supervisor's technical and administrative knowledge and skills. The test
is simply this: Does he have the answers?

Interpersonal activities that involve the use of information can
contribute substantially to good relationships. But to extend training far beyond structuring efforts in the pursuit of satisfying
relations—to the extent, for example, of having the new supervisor
imitate the style and manner of a well-liked supervisor—is ill advised. Such dramatic mimicry is likely to produce an ersatz leader
whose pretensions will be pricked in short order. And to go beyond
the effective use of information to force a participative style, model
or no model, on the new supervisor is to endow participation with
more clout in producing results necessary to industry's survival—
productivity primarily—than a hard look at the evidence would
justify. The new supervisor must get off on the right foot. He
should be respectful of employees, helpful, and communicative,
but he need not win a popularity contest in the first month.

To summarize our early training intent: we should first teach the
new supervisor the structuring aspects of his job. The use of information, along with technical and administrative procedures, will be
aimed at that objective, although these efforts are likely to have
important by-products in the way of relationships and employee
satisfaction.

Later, when procedural, technical, and communication skills have
taken hold, it is advisable for supervisors to concentrate on relationships and to decide in what aspects of their functions, and with
what employees, a more liberal use of information and a greater
degree of employee participation are indicated. We will examine
this subject at greater length when we consider the sustaining of
performance.

Interpersonal activities should be examined periodically to determine their current utility and validity. As with procedures, they can persist beyond the point of need. Even more than with procedures, they are subject to superstition; the supervisor who has experienced some satisfaction or success in the activity in the past may continue to perform the ritual even when it no longer brings satisfaction. But arbitrarily to cease such contacts may prove an unwise course. The supervisor must decide whether the by-products of an activity—succor or social satisfaction of importance to employees—are in themselves justification when the activity no longer serves its original purpose.

Finally, interpersonal activities are subject to skill development, and our training should be geared to foster that development.

Outline of Responsibilities, Functions, and Activities

The outline of responsibilities, functions, and activities presented in Table 2 can serve as a model for identifying the new supervisor's specific training needs and for planning courses, schedules, techniques, and other arrangements. This outline is typical, I believe, of first-line supervisory jobs, although the structure or nature of the jobs will vary among departments, plants, and industries; to that extent, the outline will require modification.

Background Requirements

To run the job well, the new supervisor must gain skill in performing the specified job activities. These activities represent the way the supervisor carries out his functions and meets his responsibilities, the way he maintains efficiency and quality of output and utilizes, develops, and protects his workforce. They are, in effect, the means by which the business of operating a department is conducted—the means by which, to introduce a descriptive term, the "substantive" matters of running the supervisory job are handled.

Yet, though the substantive activities are the main focus of training, it is an unwise strategy to move the new supervisor into them

(Text continues page 20.)

TABLE 2.

Supervisory responsibilities, functions, and activities.

| Responsibility | Function | Background Requirements | | Activities to Be Learned | |
		Knowledge	Skill	Procedural (Technical and Administrative)	Interpersonal
Maintaining output and efficiency of production	Monitoring production in relation to schedule; investigating and correcting output difficulties	Machinery output data Content of efficiency, production, and waste reports Stock storage and inventory system Production scheduling and control system Changes in gears or settings to achieve changes in production rate	Making changes in gears or settings affecting output Problem solving Decision making Interviewing	Review schedule data and production requirements Survey stock needs and available stock Work out machinery layout to meet output requirements Seek solution to production bottlenecks and other output problems Review production reports, machinery output figures, efficiency and waste reports; prepare production reports and keep production records	Communicate output objectives to employees Communicate output rate changes (involving machine adjustments) to machine setters or repairmen; give necessary instructions Communicate with other shifts and adjoining departments concerning production flow, output rate, and needs for necessary coordination

Monitoring operation and condition of machinery; investigating and correcting maintenance problems	Machine construction, operating principles, parts, and settings Supply parts storage and ordering system Content of efficiency reports	Operation of machines Repair of machines: settings, diagnosis Problem solving Decision making Interviewing	Conduct inspection of machinery to ensure proper maintenance and operation Seek solution to problems of malfunctioning Maintain log of repairs on equipment and machinery Order replacement parts and maintain supply	Communicate with repairmen on non-routine maintenance problems
Monitoring production costs; investigating and correcting above-standard costs	Cost factors and cost accounting system Content of and bases for cost reports	Working up cost figures for a department Problem solving Decision making Interviewing	Review cost reports for presence of problems; take remedial actions Take cost-effective actions when situations arise Compile cost data	Communicate required action to affected employees (before the fact to avoid excessive costs and after the fact to correct causes of reported excessive costs)

TABLE 2, *cont.*

| Responsibility | Function | Background Requirements | | Activities to Be Learned | |
		Knowledge	Skill	Procedural (Technical and Administrative)	Interpersonal
Maintaining quality of product	Monitoring condition of materials and quality of items produced or in process; investigating and correcting causes of substandard quality	Quality standards Material and product specifications (properties and construction) Quality testing and inspection procedures Effect on quality of such factors as machine conditions and settings Content of quality reports	Diagnosing machine problems affecting quality Conducting laboratory tests of material and product (for quality and evidence of machine problems) Problem solving Decision making Interviewing	Inspect machines for operational and maintenance features affecting quality Inspect material at various processing stages to detect immediate quality problems Review quality reports and inspection reports for evidence of problems Take remedial action when inspections or reviews reveal problems	Communicate with employees on quality problems involving them and required action by them Give directions to employees on required actions; give instruction in case of inadequate skill Communicate quality information to other shifts and adjoining departments

Maintaining employee safety and health	Monitoring physical hazards, health hazards, and unsafe acts; correcting unsafe conditions and acts	Factors in accident causation Industrial hygiene program Properties of materials used or processed OSHA provisions Motivation	Problem solving Decision making Interviewing	Make periodic inspections to spot physical hazards, health hazards, and unsafe acts Make physical changes to eliminate hazards or offset their effect Report health matters to proper authority for action Maintain orderly storage and work areas	Instruct new employees in safety and health matters Correct employees for unsafe acts; give instruction in case of lack of skill or knowledge Make sure that employees wear protection, use lockout devices, and follow other safekeeping procedures
	Reporting and investigating accidents; correcting causes of reported accidents	Compensation provisions Content of accident reports (including OSHA requirements) Factors in accident causation Motivation	Problem solving Decision making Interviewing	Report accidents and investigate causes; take remedial action Carry out follow-up procedures for remedial action Review accident reports for evidence of problems relating to jobs, work areas, machinery.	Communicate with employees on causes and corrective actions; give instruction if lack of skill or knowledge is the cause or otherwise ensure that unsafe acts are stopped
Safeguarding employees and property in security incidents	Safeguarding employees and property in security incidents	Security organization, system, and procedures		Take action to protect lives and property; report situation to designated security personnel or authorities	Communicate with affected employees on situation and actions; secure cooperation

TABLE 2, *cont.*

| Responsibility | Function | Background Requirements | | Activities to Be Learned | |
		Knowledge	Skill	Procedural (Technical and Administrative)	Interpersonal
Utilizing and compensating employees	Assigning work	Company rules and union contract provisions governing assignments, seniority, job rights, shift rights, temporary transfers, overtime distribution, and similar matters Machine layouts for workload assignments	Problem solving Decision making Interviewing	Report changes in employee status (job, shift, and so on) for personnel records	Fill job assignments at start of shift and makes changes as necessary to fill jobs and meet output needs Arrange for and distribute overtime
	Establishing and monitoring job methods	Motivation Details of approved methods on jobs Techniques for establishing or changing methods Training techniques Motivation	Establishing a job method by professional technique Interviewing	Periodically observe job methods used by employees Assist in (or conduct) methods studies on new jobs; establish method Establish new method required by product change, machinery modifications, or other adjustments	Ensure that new employees are trained in established method Ensure that employees are retrained in proper method as required Explain new methods when changes are made; ensure adequate retraining

Installing and monitoring pay standards	Details of system of establishing rates (job evaluation, time studies) Company rules and union contract provisions governing rate changes Rules governing pay in special circumstances (overtime, waiting time, reporting time, nonstandard conditions, temporary transfers) Job rates and learner rates in department Rate progression system Motivation	Conducting job evaluation and time studies Interviewing	Assist with evaluation of new or changed jobs Prepare for time studies Install new rates Periodically review earnings, changed conditions, and other factors justifying rate change study Apply wage administration rules governing special circumstances	Explain time study requirements to operators being studied Explain new rates to affected employees Explain use of modified rates in special circumstances
Administering payroll	Details of timekeeping and time-coding system Details of pay calculations (work of payroll and cost clerks, computer usage) Details of payroll deductions (for taxes, benefits, etc.) Paycheck distribution system and rules	Interviewing	Carry out timekeeping activities assigned to department See that checks are distributed to employees	Explain deductions to new employees Answer employee questions concerning gross pay or net pay and how arrived at

TABLE 2, cont.

Responsibility	Function	Background Requirements		Activities to Be Learned	
		Knowledge	Skill	Procedural (Technical and Administrative)	Interpersonal
Developing personnel and stabilizing workforce	Training and re-training employees	Principles of learning; training techniques Content of training plans and induction program Use of audiovisual and other aids Motivation (emphasis on reinforcement)	Drawing up a training plan Instructing Operating audiovisual equipment Problem solving (performance problems) Interviewing	Review new and revised training plans Diagnose learning problems	Give induction information to new employees and conduct follow-up discussions of progress Ensure that new employees are adequately trained and specific learning problems are addressed
	Monitoring employee performance; investigating and correcting causes of substandard performance	Indexes of employee performance Output and quality standards Factors related to performance Factors related to turnover and absenteeism Content of turnover and absenteeism reports Motivation (emphasis on reinforcement and sustaining performance)	Problem solving (performance problems) Decision making Interviewing	Follow up employee performance by record and observation When performance is below expectation, analyze causes and take indicated action Review absenteeism and turnover reports and analyze causes for high incidence; take remedial action	Ensure that action is taken (training, motivation, job conditions) to correct poor performance Deal with high-absentee employees

Hiring, promoting, and transferring employees	Company policies and union contract provisions governing promotion and transfer Qualification requirements for jobs EEO hiring and promotion requirements Motivation	Interviewing Decision making	Make decisions on hiring, transfer, promotion, and demotion (applying proper criteria and using pertinent procedures)	Interview applicants for hiring and promotion Discuss transfers and promotions with employees
Hearing and adjudicating complaints and grievances	Grievance procedure Company policy and union contract clauses relating to grievance handling and subjects of grievances History and focus of grievances in department EEO requirements Motivation	Problem solving Decision making Interviewing	Investigate bases of complaints or grievances; apply appropriate company rules, procedures, and contract clauses Serve as witness for higher-level steps in grievance procedure	Listen to grievances and complaints and explain position and decision
Maintaining discipline	Disciplinary rules and policy (offenses, penalties, and procedures for administering) History of disciplinary cases in department EEO requirements Motivation	Problem solving Decision making Interviewing	Investigate cases; identify offenses and apply appropriate penalties	Take disciplinary action and explain position to employee

immediately, without providing him with underlying concepts and skills, referred to in Table 2 as "background requirements." Some of this preparation is related to substantive activities and is intended to give increased meaning to the activities and to convince the new supervisor of their utility. Any efforts to control quality, for example, will be largely blind gestures and lacking in conviction unless the supervisor has firm knowledge of quality standards and product specifications. Similarly, actions to increase the efficiency of a machine are likely to be misdirected if the supervisor is unaware of the basic mechanical functioning of the machine. Again, a supervisor is hard put to take appropriate personnel actions unless he knows about company procedures, union contract provisions, and nondiscrimination requirements.

Equally important as background for acquiring skill in substantive job activities are:

1. Beginning skill in processes that we might call "vehicular" in the sense that they underpin the development of substantive skills. Examples include interviewing or communications skills, which provide a basis for developing skill in interpersonal exchanges on the job, and problem solving, which will expedite the learning of approaches to specific job situations.

2. A fundamental grasp of motivation, the "pervasive" subject present in all substantive supervisory activities involving employees.

Stress should be placed on the vehicular and pervasive subjects as background preparation for training in job activities and not as independent and self-contained topics. A supervisor is not taught to "communicate" and "motivate" in isolation. Rather, he should be trained to use the concepts and rudimentary skills in acquiring the substantive skills that represent mastery of job activities. It is through applications to job (or joblike) activities—applications sharpened and modified by pertinent training—that the "payoff" occurs.

Distinguishing among substantive, vehicular, and pervasive matters serves another purpose: to indicate that supervisory topics are not equal in purpose or value and should not be subjected to the same training arrangement.

SKILL FOR IMPROVING INSIGHT AND ATTITUDE

Some background requirements are for skills that have an indirect purpose. In certain functions we need to teach to the new supervisor skill in activities not directly performed on the supervisory job itself in order to give him greater insight into his activities. For example, if the supervisor is to ensure that machines are properly maintained and that his inspectional and instructional activities are of maximum use toward this end, he should have not only a knowledge of machine adjustments and settings but a moderate degree of skill in making such adjustments and settings and in diagnosing malfunctions. He will not repair machines himself on the job, but he must recognize whether his repairmen are performing adequately and must help spot and correct troublesome conditions that defy routine repairs. A constructive relationship with repairmen requires this sort of competency.

We must also teach the new supervisor certain background skills to convince him that the system he is administering is soundly based and equitable. For example, if he is to be effective in utilizing labor and controlling labor costs (and convincing employees), he must first be convinced himself that the system of evaluating jobs and establishing rates is a professional and defensible one. It is not enough to teach him *about* the system of evaluating jobs and making time studies; conviction is more likely to occur in the doing. Through actually evaluating jobs and conducting time studies, he will come to see that the techniques are reasonable, practical, and reliable, and that the mysterious art of performance rating is a straightforward, analytic procedure, one that he can master himself.

He will not evaluate jobs or make time studies on the job, but his contacts with employees will be more productive, since he will really know what went into the standard. In addition, he will be able to work more effectively with industrial engineers, with no need for blind acceptance (perhaps tinged with uninformed distrust) of the rates emerging from their studies. He is also more likely to identify himself with a rate once he has accepted it.

It is useful to have the new supervisor work through certain cost calculations in the system so that he has a better grasp of the cost figures for which he is held accountable or partly accountable. With this firm knowledge of what goes into the operating reports, he will be more likely to appreciate their relevance to his operation and their value in controlling costs, rather than resent them as a critical comment on his performance by "those pencil pushers who do not appreciate a supervisor's problems."

The objectives of training are usually defined as changes in knowledge, skill, and attitudes. In supervisory training (or any training, perhaps), it is questionable to work specifically on attitudes with techniques designed for that purpose alone. Aside from providing what satisfactions we can to the learner, along with information, we have very few tools for tackling attitudes. Even if we possessed the means and could transfer them to the trainer, an effort aimed exclusively at attitude would be a dubious gesture. A new supervisor is likely to have a more positive attitude if he sees his functions and the related systems, procedures, and activities as practical, reasonable, and equitable. With some functions, as suggested earlier, such appreciation on the supervisor's part is realized not through knowledge alone but through the acquisition of some degree of skill in the doing.

SKILL IN VEHICULAR SUBJECTS

In certain subjects, background skill is the beginning phase of job skill, providing a basis for generalizing skills to joblike situations and for developing more specific skills in job activities themselves. This is true of several of the vehicular skills—problem solving, decision making, and interviewing—on which many job activities will ride. Certain activities require basic models that have wide application but that underlie the approach to be taken in certain supervisory acts. In addition to understanding the models, the new supervisor should try them out in a variety of situations so that he gains some skill in the techniques and can transfer his learning to on-the-job situations and build competency in handling such situations.

Obviously, the models cannot be efficiently learned in the abstract; they must be applied. In teaching the vehicular skills, we start with the concepts of the models; and any meaningful illustrations will serve at this point to give the new supervisor "the idea." But since the objective is to develop skill, we move to applications—and in a progressive way, with matters that are increasingly pertinent to the supervisory job. In teaching background skill, we give the supervisor practice in using the model in a number of realistic supervisory situations. This practice will aid him in handling a wider variety of supervisory problems, ones reproduced from "real life," as he receives training in substantive subjects. In the process, he not only gains skill in applying the models but also sharpens the models themselves, modifying, dropping, or emphasizing certain elements so that the approaches better fit the situations he confronts; and he begins to gain skill in making such modificatons and adaptations. This classroom practice in turn prepares him for the final stage of training, when he refines and expands his skill, under the guidance of a coach, through dealing with supervisory problems on the job itself.

Problem solving and decision making are a case in point. Our goal is to teach an analytic approach to the new supervisor. It is not enough to review the framework of the model strictly in explanatory and illustrative terms, though we may start there. Our classroom objective is to develop a transferable skill and therefore requires that we run through a number of meaningful problems with our analytic procedure and move to even more pertinent and more numerous problems in substantive courses concerned with quality, efficiency, safety, and other matters. Thus we create a quick buildup of skill in handling actual problems on the job itself. As I will note again and again, on-the-job applications should be taught through coaching, a chore that proceeds much more quickly when there has been progressive classroom instruction in concepts, background skills, and substantive applications.

Interviewing is another vehicular subject that can benefit from background skill and substantive applications in a classroom setting, beyond the cognitive grasp of communication procedures and principles. The final applications comprise a good part of the supervisor's job activities; a supervisor is endlessly engaged in interpersonal contacts. Some beginning skill in getting and giving information in a realistic kind of interchange and broadened skill through role playing will promote a quick further development of skill, under coaching, in dealing with on-the-job situations that require the exchange of information.

CONCEPTS IN JOB ORGANIZATION AND MOTIVATION

In certain subjects—particularly job organization, which can be described as a vehicular subject, and motivation, a pervasive subject—background training should be largely conceptual, since the "doing" cannot really be taught outside the context of job activities.

Background training in job organization should provide the new supervisor with a conceptual framework for schedules, routines, and time utilization, within which his learned activities can operate and his specific job can be structured. In order to organize the specific job, the supervisor must have the job at hand. But the background principles will help.

As background training in motivation, the supervisor needs sound principles to guide him in his myriad contacts with employees. Motivation pervades every aspect of employee performance and behavior. As such, the subject cannot be divorced from the supervisor's substantive activities. We cannot adequately train new supervisors to motivate employees outside the context of interpersonal exchanges on training, safety, labor relations, and other substantive matters. As background, we can explain, illustrate, and discuss a motivational model and related principles designed to enhance employee performance and satisfaction. But training in applications will occur in the process of instructing the supervisor—in class with realistic cases and later in on-the-job situations—in the handling of substantive matters.

Making Effective Use of Training Techniques

The specific training techniques used to help the supervisor master the job are ones with which we are all familiar:

Classroom lectures
Classroom "action" training (discussion, modeling, and role playing)

Training in manipulative and technical skills
Consultation
Coaching

Obviously, the technique should fit the purpose. A classroom lecture is adequate to impart information, provided we assure, through questioning, that the information has been understood and, through repetition and follow-up, that it has been retained. If we wish to develop supervisory skill as well, we must use classroom "action" training and coaching.

The first point to be made about techniques, therefore, is that not all functions and related activities will call for the same treatment. With an activity that requires background knowledge and skill and training in procedures and interpersonal matters, a gamut of teaching approaches would be used, with heavy emphasis on coaching. If an activity involves a simple procedure, a less extensive treatment will serve.

Second, since skill in each activity is developmental, a single training technique will rarely suffice for mastery of the activity. We do not meet the new supervisor's needs by merely imparting information and ideas—in regard to any activity. Nor do we serve our full purpose as trainers if we concern ourselves with *what* supervisors do to perform an activity. Instead, our training must go further to encompass the "how" and the "how well"—the aspects of performance representing skill. It is our task as trainers to offer insightful help at appropriate points to build supervisory skill.

Coaching is a universal requirement for teaching activities, but additional requirements for specific activities will be dictated by an analysis of training needs. Even coaching will vary in kind and intensity and length, depending on the nature and difficulty of the activity.

The new supervisor does not quickly acquire overall job competency. It takes considerable time, under the best of training arrangements, to bring him to the point of performing every aspect of the job well—an achievement that is the objective of training and the criterion of training success. Overall skill tends to develop unevenly because of differences in the nature and complexity of activities. Through developing skill, however unevenly, in specific activities, supervisors move toward total job competency. But they do not reach that ultimate level solely by mastering the separate activities. They must also organize the job in terms of schedules, routines, and priorities so that acquired skills come into play at appropriate times and an efficiency and economy of effort are built into the job. Otherwise, the job demands, however well supervisors may meet them individually, may be overwhelming. Again, our function as trainers is to expedite the development of skill—total job skill in this case—by making distinctions among the new supervisor's needs, as we anticipate them and as they develop, and by varying the approach, timing, frequency, and extent of our training accordingly.

There are practical problems associated with arranging the training. After we analyze training needs, we must design an economical as well as effective program—giving due consideration to the possibilities of group training, for example. The program must encompass all training needs. This task requires us to examine identified needs and to develop a list of topics and a practical outline and schedule to cover them comprehensively. The functions themselves do not necessarily represent course topics or inclusive teaching regimens. Rather, we should work from the activities which must be mastered and ensure, through practical arrangements, that background knowledge and skills are imparted as required and that the development of skill in performing the activities (the substantive matters) is provided for adequately. Of course, the plan should not be so rigid that it cannot be modified to accommodate learners' rates of progress and contingencies. But to achieve full training, we must start with as comprehensive a plan as our insight and foresight can devise.

It is unrealistic to discuss training content without referring to training approaches and techniques. What we plan to teach will dictate how we teach it. The training methods should not be put aside altogether for later consideration; they should be attached to content and then set out in an orderly array which will lead logically to schedules and arrangements—the final steps in constructing a comprehensive program. If supervisors could learn all they needed to learn by simply taking a series of lecture courses, the training process could be standardized for all topics. But it is not so simple a matter. In order to bring supervisors' performance to a satisfactory level, we must help them develop a number of competencies, which differ in kind, importance, and difficulty and thus require different treatment. Moreover, there are "subskills" which must be acquired to some degree and fed into the main components at appropriate times. Finally, in planned progression, everything should be brought into mesh.

So as we examine the content of each training topic in the following chapters, we will also consider the training approaches and techniques required for efficient learning. Later we will turn our full attention to the training process, examining suggested outlines and schedules for the classroom training and on-the-job coaching by which we may confront all the new supervisor's training needs and move him to mastery of the full job.

CHAPTER 2

The Substantive Subjects

S UBSTANTIVE TOPICS are subjects that deal directly with the procedural and interpersonal activities which, in effect, comprise the supervisor's job. In our training efforts we may start from different bases and take different channels, but ultimately we are concerned with seeing that the new supervisor's on-the-job activities are effective in regard to:

Output and maintenance of machinery and equipment
Cost control
Quality control
Safety and health of employees
Utilizing and compensating employees
Labor relations
Skills training
Induction training

These are the substantive topics we will examine in detail in this chapter. We will not bother, therefore, with such airy issues as planning, delegating, directing, controlling, communicating, and other global matters except insofar as fragments of them show up as definable, teachable, and pertinent job activities.

Output and Maintenance of Machinery and Equipment

The fact that the supervisor accomplishes tasks by working through others does not eliminate the need for him to become reasonably proficient in what the others do—in operating and maintaining the machinery and equipment in his department. The supervisor must oversee the training of employees and in some situations directly engage in such training himself. He must evaluate the work of employees and insightfully attack operational and maintenance problems. These activities are sufficient argument for training supervisors in the job skills (at least in major job classifications) of their employees.

To accomplish this purpose, we must give the supervisor classroom instruction and, if practical, vestibule instruction (in a training room where machinery has been made available) in operational principles and in machinery settings, adjustments, and diagnostic procedures. Even more important, we must provide one-on-one instruction in operating and repairing the machinery and enough directed experience to ensure reasonable competency. Supervisors need not reach the piece-rate level of output of an operator or match the skill of their better repairmen, but they do need more than observational or "book" knowledge. A look at employees in action and a run through a manual will not serve. As background for monitoring output and efficiency of operation and for the technical supervision of employees, supervisors need more than a greenhorn's skill in running the jobs in their department.

They also need knowledge of the production systems—scheduling, production reporting, parts purchasing, and so forth—and some background in problem solving and interviewing. Skill in the specific activities involved in monitoring, scheduling, troubleshooting, and other functions can then be acquired through coaching on the job.

Controlling Costs

Most companies, especially those in highly competitive industries, will surround a supervisor with cost data. If a standard cost system is used, for example, supervisors will receive or have access to periodic reports, by process or cost center, on labor, supplies, raw materials, and other elements of cost. And the reports will relate the expenditures at each cost center to a standard figure representing acceptable control of costs for the achieved output. Supervisors are also likely to receive a machine efficiency report that compares machine operating time or output to a 100 percent base (no downtime) or to a base less a standard time allowance for repairing and servicing. Quality and waste reports—showing actual figures and percentages of standard allowance—are usually included in the package of periodic reports on operational results. In most cases, these reports are issued at weekly intervals.

The reports are a measure of what the supervisor's department (and the supervisor himself, to the extent of his influence on the indexes) is accomplishing. They are also the beginning evidence of operational problems; with accompanying diagnosis they serve as the basis for actions initiated by the supervisor or directed by the department head, and are indications of the effectiveness of such actions. As a significant signal for departmental actions and a measure of their success, the reports should be a primary tool in managing a department or subdepartment. Thus the supervisor needs to be given an intimate knowledge of what the figures in the report really mean, including a probing behind the figures to the accounting system which produces them. Such training is aimed not at making accountants of supervisors but at putting enough meaning into the reports, through a comprehensive look at how they are derived, to convince supervisors that they can rely on the data and to ensure that they constructively use the reports as a managing aid.

Clearly, first-line supervisors will have less influence on the system than department heads. For example, they are not likely to be directly involved in final budgeting, which is usually the province of the department head and plant manager in collaboration with the accounting staff. But supervisors will probably be consulted by the department head as to their needs and asked for budgetary suggestions or recommendations. In any event, they need to know what goes into the budget and why; their actions will inevitably help determine whether the department operates as planned. So in class, for compelling reasons, we should teach the new supervisor the system in some detail, though it may be heavy going, concentrating on the operational reports and emphasizing their utility as a managing aid.

On the job, the supervisor proceeds from analyzing the cost reports to diagnosing specific reasons for failure to meet the cost standards and taking remedial action. As preparation for such activities, our classroom sessions should review operational reports and supporting data and then focus on what the reports and data reveal as possible leads to causative factors that require attention. The background training given in problem solving will come into play in such discussions.

But the reports are a numerical statement of what happened last week. As indicated, they do flag the presence of a problem and provide a starting point for improving off-standard figures in the immediate future. Thus the supervisor takes steps to clear up an existing problem or last week's problem—but after the fact, as a sort of repair operation. A much more economic and efficient approach is to prevent the problems from arising. To help supervisors take preventive measures, we should focus our training on current situations, dealing with day-by-day, cost-effective decisions that will lead to acceptable control figures. Such "preventive" teaching can be undertaken in class by presenting a number of realistic cases in which the supervisor must choose among actions with varying degrees of cost effectiveness. An example:

> There are five major machines in your subdepartment. The workforce on your shift includes five machine operators, one to each machine; three complementary employees (service personnel) for each machine; and a repairman assigned to all five machines.
>
> *Your situation:* One of the machine operators fails to show up. Everyone else is there.

Questions for decision. What would you do:
1. If neither the repairman nor any of the complementary employees could run the machine?
2. If the repairman could run the machine at standard output?
3. If the repairman could run the machine at below-standard output?

Discussion of such cases can sharpen the supervisor's decision-making ability and set the stage for the further development of skill in making similar decisions, under coaching, on the job itself.

Training in cost control can be initiated by classroom discussion of cost problems, remedial action, and preventive action, undergirded by an earlier classroom examination of the cost system and its reports. But, as in other functions, coaching in the day-by-day activities of the job is what it takes to move supervisors to the point where they are ready to act competently on their own. Supervisors must interpret the reports pertinent to their job and learn to take the appropriate actions to correct problems or prevent their occurrence.

Objections are sometimes raised to proceeding very far with training in cost control, on the grounds that we are thus preparing the supervisor to "beat the system." There is no doubt that certain knowledgeable supervisors have made such attempts. Thus a supervisor may overbudget personnel in order to keep labor cost figures in the black. Or, gambling that the plant manager is more concerned with machine efficiency or output than labor cost, a supervisor may achieve high efficiency and output by overstaffing. Or the department head may engage in such ruses as having supervisors start machines a few hours before the first shift of the week begins and keeping them running a few hours after the last shift ends (to be turned off by the supervisors). In this way, several hours of production from unattended machines artificially inflate the record of output for the period of a "normal" week.

Potential abuses of the system are not justification for failing to teach its legitimate application. It is not possible to teach integrity, but a good coverage of the system should convince the supervisor of the advantage of using it in the way it was designed to be used.

The major caution is to ensure, as best we can, that cost figures are specifically and immediately identifiable with supervisory actions. If they are beyond supervisory control or too long delayed, cost reports are of limited value to supervisors in managing their operation or, as we will see later, as a feedback device in learning how to manage.

Quality Control

Through classroom presentation, with product samples and other illustrations, we can teach the basic facts of quality standards, product specifications, and material characteristics and working properties. We can also review in class the system established by the organization to control quality through the collaboration of line and staff, informing the new supervisor about such components of the system as setting standards; monitoring them through tests, inspections, and reinspections; and reporting and giving feedback on quality data.

But, again, simply knowing about standards and the quality control system will not fully meet the new supervisor's needs. Laboratory testing is often intimately associated with control of in-process quality. Thus, in textile yarn manufacturing, laboratory tests not only reveal quality problems but point to the roll or gear of the particular machine causing the trouble. In a matter of such importance, the supervisor should operate the testing equipment, under instruction, long enough to understand the exact nature of the information generated by the tests and should be given experience, again under instruction, in replacing or adjusting the mechanical parts identified by the tests as sources of poor quality. In the normal course of the job, supervisors will not conduct tests or perform the mechanical acts, but if such testing and correcting are at the heart of controlling quality in the department, supervisors should have an intimate "hands on" grasp of how they work.

Supervisors also need an experience-based grasp of in-process inspecting within the department. They should acquire substantial skill in applying standards under operating conditions—in perceiving defects and in classifying, grading, or judging them, according to what the inspection requires. Further, since quality is the source of recurring problems in a production department, new supervisors must be given problem-solving and decision-making models for getting at causes and remedies. Finally, since correction can usually be made only through people, they need to know something about motivation.

These are largely background needs. Beyond the training required to meet such needs, the supervisor should receive coaching in on-the-job quality control activities, primarily in inspecting machines and material, reviewing quality records, and taking remedial action.

Safety and Health

There are a number of safety procedures new supervisors must learn. Since they conduct periodic inspections to detect hazards, they must know not only what to look for but how to conduct the survey perceptively and efficiently. In addition, they frequently fill out various forms—a first-aid form when minor injuries are treated in the department, more comprehensive forms (company and governmental) on cases requiring professional medical attention, and a state government form in regard to compensable cases. Reporting and recording requirements are established by the company, by the state for compensation purposes, and by the federal government through OSHA. The supervisor not only must be familiar with the information required by the forms but must become adept at collecting the information and recording it.

In training the new supervisor in safety and health procedures, therefore, it is necessary to move from factual coverage to practice. This process can begin with classroom analysis and reporting of accident information and with class-related assignments involving inspections of operating departments. Ultimately, the training will require on-the-job coaching.

Yet, since safety deals with life itself, the training must be solidly founded on valid theories of the causes of accidents. We should focus on giving new supervisors an enlightened view of accident causation—at least to the point of introducing them to general research findings and specific results from investigations conducted in the plant. With such a grounding in cause-and-effect relationships, the new supervisor is likely to move more securely into action and to appreciate the value of data bearing on causes. Otherwise, safety procedures become routine gestures, divorced from the basic intent of preventing accidents. The inspection reports may fill files rather than spur the correction of physical hazards.

Similarly, the supervisor should view the completion of accident forms in an analytical light, as serving the purpose of preventing future accidents; the data must be aimed at identifying causes. We must not minimize the importance of other considerations in reporting. Certainly the matter of Workers' Compensation—its administration requirements and schedules of awards—is important and a legitimate subject for training in itself. But the major intent of filling out accident forms is to prevent accidents. The supervisor must view this activity as an investigation of causes, using the results to direct him to meaningful action.

The examination of accident causation should take into account the interaction of factors preceding the accident, the effect of temporary stress, and other insightful findings emerging from current research. In handling accidents on the job, supervisors must be guided, first of all, by the conviction that a superficial look at causes or a reliance on folklore is not a reliable basis for remedial action. And we must ensure that the action is not a superficial correction (such as cautioning the employee to "be more careful," "take it slow," or "pay more attention") that does not deal with the underlying problem. Truly remedial actions are especially difficult to take when the cause lies primarily in unsafe acts and has a motivational aspect involving the sacrifice of safety to meet other needs or the reaction to frustration.

The new supervisor can be given insight into accident causation through classroom lectures and practice in diagnosing the causes of accidents through case studies. As training in the handling of unsafe acts, we can add role playing of corrective interviews to our classroom treatment, since interpersonal contacts are heavily involved in such cases. Such classroom measures help substantially to build the new supervisor's skill in making a rounded attack on unsafe acts—an attack which includes determining underlying causes, planning remedial action, and conducting interviews to determine causes and courses of action and to initiate corrective action.

Then supervisors need coaching on the job in analyzing accident causes and taking remedial action. They should direct their corrective measures heavily at unsafe acts, since these contribute to a high percentage of total accidents. We are well advised to devote most of our safety training time to "handling" such acts—not only those which result in injury but near-misses as well.

Currently supervisors are less involved with matters of employee health than with accident prevention, but health is of increasing concern to state and federal governments (with OSHA requirements focusing on health as well as safety) and to industrial organizations. Such concern will inevitably be translated into increased activity at the supervisory level. Even at this time, the supervisor must be made aware of OSHA provisions, standards related to materials processed or substances used in the processing, environmental conditions (such as dust and noise), company responsibilities, and employee responsibilities. Supervisors must know about the characteristics and possible effects of materials and must be alert to their possible noxious effect on employees. And they must ensure that the procedures instituted to protect employees from health and physical hazards—the wearing of ear plugs, masks, goggles, safety shoes, and other protective gear—are actually in effect. Supervisors must serve not only as teachers and enforcers but as examples as well. If they themselves fail to wear proper protection in designated areas, they will be ineffective in compelling compliance among employees, no matter what their persuasive powers or level of authority.

Classroom lectures can teach new supervisors health-related provisions and procedures and materials characteristics. And role playing can help them become proficient in dealing with employee violations of health rules. Our chief reliance, in teaching the "doing," will be on coaching in the job itself.

Industrial management is becoming increasingly concerned with security, a development that will inevitably be translated into supervisory action. In training the new supervisor, we can describe the company's or plant's security organization, system, and procedures for protecting personnel, product, and physical property, with emphasis on the role the supervisor is expected to play. Communicating with security personnel and other responsible authorities is an especially crucial activity and should be heavily stressed. And we can discuss certain common or predictable emergency situations, using incidents that have occurred in the plant or company as cases to prepare the new supervisor for making appropriate responses. Beyond such training efforts, our chief hope lies in the supervisor's emotional control and exercise of intelligence in the face of crisis. Having at least an idea of what to do may help him in both regards.

Companies that experience frequent or highly dangerous emergencies need to go further with their security training of supervisors (and operators as well), resorting to drills or rehearsals given often enough to bring about genuine learning and to cover the full cycle of activities in each emergency situation: perceiving discriminatively the signs of trouble and taking the appropriate actions.

Utilizing and Compensating Employees

Utilizing and compensating employees, as a supervisory function, is essentially a matter of making sure that employees perform jobs by adhering to efficient methods and that they are equitably paid for what they do. The means are largely matters of industrial engineering.

Industrial engineering, among many things, is concerned with defining effective job methods—motion patterns and sequences of steps—and with establishing and maintaining a compensation system which relates to job requirements and the level of job performance. The supervisor is also vitally concerned with these matters, and it is chiefly in regard to them that he must receive training in industrial engineering.

In some cases supervisors, as a job duty, actively engage in establishing job methods and accompanying layout. They then should receive thorough training in methods analysis, through class explanation of techniques, classroom exercises, and perhaps assignments involving visits to production departments, and on-the-job activities under coaching. When job methods are determined exclusively by industrial engineers, as a minimum the supervisor must critically evaluate the proposed methods, install them, and train employees in them (or supervise such training). In addition, the supervisor must monitor the methods used by employees to be sure they are adhering to efficient methods and must also detect any significant changes in job content, requirements, or conditions that require a revision of method or invalidate the rate or workload. Although supervisors will not need as much method-setting skill as industrial engineers, they need enough of it to handle these activities professionally; otherwise they are likely to function rather blindly as agents of the Industrial Engineering Department.

In any case, supervisors must be thoroughly trained in job methods in their department, not only by observation but (in association with their training function) by actual performance, at least in the major job classifications. Job methods can be reviewed in class discussions and by observation of employees either on site or through TV tapes or films. The background skill in performing the jobs requires on-site training.

Supervisors do not engage directly in establishing rates. But they must assist industrial engineers in arranging for studies and obtaining proper study conditions and in explaining the resulting standards to employees. Such activities require background skill in evaluating jobs and making time studies. As discussed earlier, training in "doing" can also convince the supervisor that the studies are valid and the results equitable. In large part, training can be given in a classroom setting, through evaluation of common jobs familiar to new supervisors and time studies of contrived tasks or filmed jobs in addition to observed operational jobs.

Of course, supervisors should be well informed about the results of evaluation and time studies in their department. They should know the complete rate structure in the department—the piece-rate and day-rate levels of earnings per hour in various jobs—and the relative positions of the jobs in the evaluation hierarchy. Decisions on promotion, transfer, and demotion would be blind gestures without such information. In addition, supervisors should know the workloads of the jobs under their jurisdiction. The wage rate schedule and data on workloads are available in the departmental office, of course, but questions on these and other issues related to rates and workload come up repeatedly on the production floor. The supervisor's competency becomes a subject of employee speculation if he beats a path to and from the office. Supervisors are not expected to have all the facts at their immediate command, with no need for confirmation, but they should have a substantial store of knowledge. Such knowledge can be acquired by consulting with department heads and by studying source data early in the supervisory assignment.

It is difficult for supervisors to explain the results of individual time studies to employees, especially when the workload is increased or the rate per piece decreased. These are likely outcomes of engineering studies when improvements in machinery or methods have occurred, though the amount of actual work required of the operator for the same money may remain the same. In order to explain how more output requires no more work, the supervisor must have an intimate knowledge of the bases for the new rate or workload standards and a thorough understanding of the time-study techniques. Such explanatory skill can be developed initially through classroom role-playing exercises based on realistic cases of standards changes and can be enhanced through on-the-job activities. But efficient development may depend on the coaching given the new supervisor in handling such troublesome communication. Training in explaining the reasons for new time studies can follow a similar course.

WAGE ADMINISTRATION

Perhaps the most complex pay-related supervisory activity is the determination of the pay rate that should apply in unusual circumstances. The supervisor must know the rules applying to the full range—and it is a wide one—of special rates: reporting time, waiting time, overtime, rates applying to temporary assignment to another job or to supervisory chores, bonus pay for instructing, make-up pay to guaranteed levels for learners on piece-rate jobs who fail to make the rate in output, progressive rates for learners in day-rate jobs as they advance to full rate, rate ranges for complex jobs or maintenance jobs that require advancement through a hierarchy of skill levels, bonuses for quality, special allowances for off-standard conditions, and guaranteed rates during new workload or rate installations. In many companies the list is long and the rules multiple, and supervisors do not have unlimited time to answer employees, although they usually have ample time to make payroll notations.

The rules applying to special rates and their appropriate application can be taught through classroom lectures. The training material would include union contract clauses on rate matters and the company's written payroll procedures. The new supervisor can begin to acquire skill in pay-related activities through classroom discussion of a variety of case studies calling for decisions on rates to be paid. Beyond the classroom, coaching in on-the-job situations will expedite learning.

Since pay is often the key to an employee's satisfaction, the new supervisor must be moved quickly—and far enough with cases and on-the-job situations—toward mastery of this activity.

In monitoring earnings, the supervisor must be alert to extraordinary changes in group earnings that may justify invoking union contract clauses or other provisions for restudying workloads and rates.

PAYROLL PROCEDURES

The supervisor's involvement in payroll procedures will depend on the extent to which timekeepers, payroll clerks, computers, or other personnel and aids are used in payroll calculations and administrative procedures. But even in an automated system, the supervisor is usually held accountable for the basic data—the timebook or similar record of hours worked by each employee, shown by task number and by a notation signifying payment of special rates. And the supervisor must clarify any questions the employee has about his paycheck—gross or net amounts, deductions, and so forth. Instruction in the content of time records, the payroll process, and the entries on the paycheck and stub can be covered by lecture; but the explanation of how we get from gross pay through the various deductions, voluntary and compulsory, to net or take-home pay can benefit from classroom practice. One of the first chores the new supervisor should be assigned, under coaching on the job, is his timekeeping activity.

A supervisor is also involved in distributing paychecks, a simple matter but one that requires a knowledge of rules for issuing paychecks when the employee is absent on the pay date or has just been separated from employment with pay due him or when other unusual circumstances arise. Rules that apply to the company or plant as a whole can be explained in group classroom sessions. Practices unique to a department are best taught on the job.

Labor Relations

The supervisor, first of all, needs to know the rules of the game in supervising employees. These are specified in company policies and procedures, in the union contract if the plant is unionized, and in government regulations. Thus the union contract and the company policy guide become the basic textbooks for training. An interpretation manual that cites past cases as precedents, clause by clause, along with rulings from grievance or arbitration decisions is a useful supplement.

These provisions and the clarifying illustrations can be adequately taught by lectures. The classroom work should then proceed to case studies that give the new supervisor practice in applying the appropriate contract or policy clauses to various situations. Classroom training can then be extended to role playing to give the new supervisor practice in the face-to-face handling of employee complaints or grievances that challenge the supervisor's decision. The supervisor can also be given practice in mock grievance cases carried to higher levels and to arbitration.

Finally, on-the-job coaching in labor relations activities, procedural and interpersonal, is required in the department itself. Such coaching should continue for a rather extensive period, since labor relations problems are numerous and complex. They involve such issues as seniority (and associated rights such as job and shift),

transfers, promotions, demotions, hours, overtime, holidays, vacation, and leaves of absence. (Training in certain aspects of pay is
best given in an industrial engineering context, such as utilization
and compensation of employees, rather than under labor relations.
These aspects include the establishment and revision of pay
standards—workload and rate—and the provisions on determining
rates in extraordinary circumstances.) As supervisors find out
rather quickly, many on-the-job problems do not lend themselves
to a "programmed" solution by direct application of a clause or
rule. Often the contract clause or policy statement does not fit
exactly or cover all circumstances.

ADMINISTERING DISCIPLINE

The training of new supervisors in administering discipline
should follow a similar progression. First, the rules and penalties
contained in the disciplinary policy should be explained. Then case
studies should be examined to help new supervisors identify the
applicable rules being violated and the appropriate penalties. With
certain kinds of offenses—absenteeism is a prime example—the
decision is not clear-cut, and the supervisor's training should include a discussion of ameliorating conditions or circumstances for
guidance. The supervisor should then role-play face-to-face interchanges in disciplinary cases.

All these approaches can be carried out in the classroom. But
coaching on the job is the crucial final requirement—for a long
enough time to ensure that the new supervisor can deal with the
fuzzy cases as well as the more obvious ones.

It is in the context of handling disciplinary cases and grievances
that the supervisor's concept of authority comes into play, and both
the classroom instructor and the on-the-job coach should be concerned with how authority should be expressed. Distinctions
should be made explicitly between situations that are a threat to the
supervisor's authority and those that are not. New supervisors
should be made to realize that their authority is not threatened by
requests or complaints or grievances or by the innocent or unknow-
ing violation of a rule. They need not overreact to preserve their
prerogatives in such cases. In a grievance, the indicated course is a

thorough and unemotional look at the situation, examining exactly what happened and the defined rights involved. Of course, immediate action is often required. But supervisors must realize that if they need to act quickly, before completing an investigation, their decision will be based not on a full development of the facts but on some degree of inference, and that it is an unwise expression of authority and indeed an undermining of authority to persist in a decision that the emerging facts will not support. A new supervisor may feel that his authority is undercut by his own boss if his decision is reversed at a higher level in the grievance procedure when more facts are brought to bear on the case. This point of view may arise from the misconception that supervisory decisions are absolute dictums, however arrived at, and that a supervisor's authority makes them inviolable.

Of course, the authority inherent in the supervisory job is considerable. But it is circumscribed by the union contract, government requirements, and the company's own policies and procedures. Within that framework, which must be thoroughly understood, new supervisors must be taught to tread their way on the basis of facts, using whatever information is available for a quick decision if necessary but keeping an open mind to the emergence of further evidence—whether it confirms their original decision or suggests the need for a new one.

Situations involving insubordination—a willful violation of an understood and reasonable rule without mitigating circumstances—are indeed a challenge to the supervisor's authority. Here, too, the supervisor must develop the facts. Indeed, since insubordination is usually subject to discharge, many companies require a fact-finding period, during which time the employee is suspended, before a final decision is made. But new supervisors should understand the difference between this sort of confrontation and a grievance over a matter of employee rights. They must be trained to use the available sanctions with discretion.

EQUAL OPPORTUNITY

The training of new supervisors in equal rights should follow the same progression from knowledge to action recommended for other labor relations matters. We begin by explaining the legal provisions established by federal law and executive order and the related rules and regulations issued by executive agencies— primarily the Equal Employment Opportunity Commission, the Department of Labor, and the Civil Service Commission. We should also include an outline of the company's Affirmative Action program. Cautious restraint is required in explaining the legal provisions, since they are voluminous. Here is an abbreviated list:

Federal Legislation
> Equal Pay Act of 1963
> Title VII (prohibiting discrimination in employment) of the Civil Rights Act of 1964
> Equal Employment Opportunity Act of 1972
> Age Discrimination in Employment Act of 1967 (and Amendments of 1978)
> Age Discrimination Act of 1975
> Rehabilitation Act of 1973

Executive Orders
> E.O. 11246 (Government Contractors and Subcontractors)— applies to any contractor with a government contract of $10,000 or more
> E.O. 11141 (Age Discrimination)
> E.O. 11914 (Nondiscrimination with Respect to the Handicapped in Federally Assisted Programs)

Regulations and Rules
> Uniform Guidelines on Employee Selection Procedure (EEOC, Civil Service Commission, Department of Justice, Department of Labor)

The intent is to make new supervisors aware of legal requirements—and the teeth in them—so that they do not naively assume an uncircumscribed authority to do what they please despite what "the piece of paper" says. On the other hand, there is perhaps a more important consideration: we need to indicate clearly and convincingly that the legal requirements still leave room for choice of action and exercise of supervisory judgment. The danger, compounded if we overwhelm supervisors with legal data, is that they will despair of framing their actions and decisions within the legal requirements. Many supervisors who traditionally share jurisdiction in hiring or give final approval abandon that responsibility and resignedly accept the first candidate referred to them by the employment office. If the candidate can work on the designated shift and has transportation to the plant, he is accepted as "qualified."

To aid the supervisor in handling questions of discrimination, we should first explain the major legal provisions pertinent to the supervisor's job, using them to launch a discussion of supervisory actions in various situations. The major emphasis in training should be on what the supervisor can and should do in a number of circumstances. Discussion of realistic cases is the indicated technique. The cases should cover a wide range of situations, since nondiscrimination requirements affect not only hiring but numerous other personnel or personnel-related activities, including promotion, transfers, overtime, discipline, pay, and training. In applications that require interpersonal contact (complaints or explanation of decisions, for example), role playing is a useful technique.

Ultimately, the setting for training is on the job itself, where the new supervisor should be coached in handling questions of discrimination. The coaching should be extensive, since equal rights is an integral or ancillary consideration in almost every personnel decision the supervisor makes. Moreover, the legal requirements apply to a wide range of employees; discrimination is forbidden not only on the basis of race, religion, and national origin but also on the basis of sex and age. In addition, the handicapped and the Vietnam veterans are receiving increased attention as guidelines and regulations begin to emerge from federal legislation and executive orders.

Trainers would be hard put to develop their own comprehensive classroom training package on equal opportunity. Fortunately, useful materials and programs are available from outside commercial sources. There is no substitute, however, for specific company guidance. Though interagency differences may have been resolved, the government guidelines on employment leave many unanswered questions and are subject, in their application, to a variety of policy decisions among operating companies. Each company should arrive at its best interpretation and should then set clear standards for employing and promoting employees in various jobs. These selection standards should be explained to supervisors, and applications should then be taught through case studies and coaching.

The company should set procedures and standards. Supervisors are in an untenable position if they are left to interpret complex guidelines on their own or to rely on the interpretations of outsiders (either those involved in the training or those whose material is used in the training) that are not specific to the supervisor's operation or job.

TURNOVER AND ABSENTEEISM

Finally, the new supervisor should be trained in handling problems of turnover and absenteeism. These topics are sometimes subsumed under the heading of labor relations, which is acceptable, and sometimes taught as separate courses in themselves, which is questionable. Factors affecting turnover and absenteeism encompass a good part of what a supervisor does to run his department effectively. How, therefore, can we teach him in a limited course how to control turnover and absenteeism?

A more reasonable approach, it would appear, is to give the supervisor background knowledge, examining the turnover and absenteeism reports and how they are derived and the findings from sound research studies appearing in the literature and from studies conducted, if any, by the company itself.* Classroom lectures can accomplish this chore in short order.

* See Lyman W. Porter and Richard M. Steers, "Organizational, Work, and Personal Factors in Employee Turnover and Absenteeism," *Psychological Bulletin,* Vol. 80, No. 2 (1973), pp. 151–176, for an excellent summary of research studies. Findings are discussed in relation to organizationwide factors of pay, promotion, and organizational size; immediate work environmental factors of supervisory style (consideration, equity of treatment, recognition, feedback, job goals, supervisory length of experience), work-unit size, and peer group interaction; job content factors of task repetitiveness, job autonomy and responsibility, and role clarity; and a number of personal factors. The summary points to the central importance of "met expectations" in the employee's decision to stay or leave. The point of view, somewhat popularly held, that turnover and absenteeism have exactly the same causes is not supported by this summary. However, fewer conclusions are possible concerning the effect of the factors on absenteeism than on turnover because of the relatively few studies on absenteeism.

At this point, turnover and absenteeism should lose their identity as course subjects and take their proper place as loose indications of how well the supervisor handles those substantive activities that are likely to influence job satisfaction—notably, induction, skills training, control of job conditions, and solving of performance problems. It is on these substantive activities, and the underlying vehicular and pervasive subjects, that we should focus our training efforts if we expect the new supervisor to control absenteeism and turnover. We prepare him with an understanding of a model of motivation and with skills in inducting and training employees and in monitoring the operation and maintenance of machinery and equipment. Through such efforts the supervisor can expect to influence turnover and absenteeism to some extent. And if other factors are at play, the problem-solving model we have provided will help the supervisor identify causes.

Supervisors should take a relatively modest stance, since there are factors in turnover and absenteeism over which they have little or no control. It is important that they realize their limitations. Nevertheless, their influence is still substantial, and they should carry out those activities within their jurisdiction that are likely to reduce turnover and absenteeism. In doing what they can, it is important that supervisors start with a solid grasp of true contributing causes, standing fast against folklore and pet solutions. Supervisors are well advised to survey their situation carefully to avoid being caught up in gimmicky campaigns that are likely to be misdirected and to have short-lived results.

Skills Training

A supervisor who believes that training is merely an exercise in common sense is in a poor position to carry out skills training in his department. Training, properly regarded, is a professional function with a body of knowledge to undergird its approaches and with specific skills to make the approaches work.

The body of background knowledge which the supervisor should be taught first is concerned not with training but with learning as the essential phenomenon to be understood. We should give the supervisor an understanding of (1) what happens in job learning in regard to the fundamental processes of stimulus discrimination and response differentiation (perceiving what needs to be responded to and making efficient responses) and of (2) how principles of learning can affect these processes. It is only at this point that we should focus on training—that is, on those arrangements and techniques, solidly based in learning theory, that will facilitate the learning process. Training exists only to aid learning, and it should not be taught as an administrative system independent of its function.

Supervisors should understand the efficacy of training arrangements that involve breaking down the job into tasks or subtasks of appropriate size to serve as units of skill for training purposes, length and spacing of practice, and conditions conducive to the transfer of skills. They should also understand the instructional techniques of explanation, demonstration, cueing, feedback, and reinforcement. Supervisors should be firmly instructed in the developmental nature of manipulative skills, in what takes place as these skills progressively improve, and in the steps they and their instructors can take to move the development along.

All these points can be picked up cognitively through lectures. But supervisors need more. Even if they do not personally draw up training plans for jobs, they need insight into what should go into such plans—an insight that only experience in drawing up a plan can bring about. So as background skill supervisors should be able to devise a training plan that utilizes learning principles and the arrangements and techniques which put the principles to work. In addition, since supervisors will probably be doing some direct training, they should acquire sound skill in the instructional techniques of explanation, demonstration, cueing, feedback, and reinforcement. Even if new employees are trained primarily by instructors within the department, supervisors must themselves possess substantial competency in instructing to oversee such activities. This competency can be acquired through teaching simple tasks in the classroom and teaching specific tasks, under the guidance of a coach, in departmental jobs themselves.

We perform a disservice for the new supervisors if we assume that all they need to carry out their training function is a little instruction in the simple JIT steps. Such a minimal gesture creates the false impression that job learning is a simple and short-term process and understates what supervisors can do to help the learning along.

Beyond the beginning stages of training employees, the supervisor must take appropriate steps when the learner's progress levels off and when difficulties occur in the performance of experienced employees. Of course, supervisors must first be aware of trouble. In the case of new employees, they should evaluate performance periodically for signs of difficulty. In the case of experienced employees, they should systematically review output or earnings data to detect the presence of problems. If the problem is validly one of skill deficiency, supervisors are ill advised to take a blunderbuss approach. Rather, they should analyze the learning problem to identify the specific trouble and then take the training approach indicated.

The diagnosis of learning problems is no simple task. The query should be far reaching: Is it a matter of method, speed, job organization, inability to cope with unusual conditions, or what? If supervisors focus correctly on one of these factors, they must extend their inquiry to pinpoint the precise cause. For example, if methods errors are found, the remedy may require more than a simple admonition to "stop doing it that way." Such a prescription is likely to be both inadequate and premature, because the specific cause of the difficulty may be still undetermined. Supervisors cannot hope to cure a learning problem if they dismiss it with a simple reference to "method." The cause of the problem may lie in the trainee's reason for doing things his way; the wrong method is probably his uninformed way of solving his difficulties so that the job may be performed somehow. The cause lies in whatever necessitated the excessive or erroneous motions.

Similarly, if the difficulty is correctly identified as lack of speed, it is not enough simply to urge greater effort. The specific problem may be an inefficient use of feedback, preventing a quick transition from one subtask to another or a simultaneous performance of subtasks. So it should go: specific remedies for specific problems.

In training advanced learners and retraining experienced employees, the new supervisor needs proficiency in analyzing performance, a thorough knowledge of job methods, and an adeptness at interpreting data and making observations in order to spot problems and discern their general causes. And if the problem concerns learning, the supervisor needs the diagnostic skill to pin down the specific problem and its causes, the discriminative ability to fit training techniques to causes, and the instructional skill to execute the techniques effectively. Mastery of such multiple and difficult skills is essential in dealing with advanced trainees and experienced personnel, because the supervisor is likely to be drawing primarily on his own resources at such late stages of employee development. The time for broad and comprehensive training, in which job instructors are often used, has passed. It is now time for problem-centered training. If the supervisor is fortunate enough to be able to call instructors back into action, he will have to direct their efforts. But he is more likely to be forced to rely solely on his own skills to carry him through the full sweep of performance improvement.

How can we train the supervisor to cope with learning problems of employees? The nature of learning problems and appropriate techniques for addressing them can be covered in classroom lectures, followed by classroom discussion of related case studies to sharpen the supervisor's selection of remedial training techniques.* Supervisors will also need direct coaching, in a production department, in diagnosing the learning problems of employees and in giving the indicated help.

Induction Training

Induction training involves helping employees adjust to their job duties, requirements, and conditions, primarily by giving them the information they need. The same process may be called orientation. Whatever we call it, it is not a simple introduction accomplished on the first day or first few days on the job. A job is a

---

* See James E. Gardner, *Helping Employees Develop Job Skill: A Casebook of Training Approaches* (Washington, D.C.: The Bureau of National Affairs, 1976). A number of such cases are cited, along with other material pertinent to training new supervisors in the skills of training employees.

large thing, and adjustment takes time. As the employee moves further into the job, new vistas are revealed—and new adjustments are required.

It is difficult, as evident from the definition, to separate induction from hiring and training. Fortunately, it is not necessary to make fine distinctions; the important consideration is that we teach activities in a meaningful context. Induction begins before the employee is hired and continues, primarily through discussions of progress, until the employee reaches an acceptable and relatively stable level of performance. In some departments first-line supervisors do not interview job candidates, but in almost every case they are an early source of information for the new employee, and they stay abreast of the employee's progress.

New supervisors should be taught in depth the various topics they need to explain to new employees, and also the schedule for covering such items. Lectures will serve for this purpose. Role playing in class can then be used to give the supervisor practice in transmitting these items in such a way as to make them understood.

New supervisors also need training in conducting periodic discussions of progress and performance with the new employee. Through lectures, they can be instructed in the system for collecting information on performance and the meaning of such information. However, action training is the greatest necessity. Role playing will help the supervisor develop skill in holding reviews, aided by a procedural framework to guide the course of the interview. A logical sequence of steps for conducting such reviews is shown below. It should be noted, however, that the supervisor's evolving skill does not reside in a mechanical adherence to this step-by-step procedure. The supervisor must learn to carry out the separate steps effectively and must become adept at diagnosing which steps are most pertinent to the employee's specific situation and concentrating on them.

1. *Survey of results.* Did the supervisor have enough objective data or other sound evidence? Did the employee accept the evidence as valid?
2. *Evaluation of results.* Did the supervisor and the employee

reach agreement on the level of performance or progress the results pointed to?

3. *Search for causes of poor results.* If the results indicated the presence of a problem, did the supervisor explore sources? With input from the employee? Did they agree on the nature of the problem and its probable cause?

4. *Planning remedial action.* Did the supervisor determine a course of action? Did the trainee contribute? Was the trainee's acceptance assured? Were provisions made for follow-up (for confirming causes if practical, for monitoring events, and for meeting foreseeable contingencies)?

A discussion without an outcome or at least satisfactory closure will be inconsequential or counterproductive. In their reviews, supervisors should call into play what they have learned in other contexts about diagnosing performance and learning problems and devising remedies. As with other activities, coaching on the job is a necessary extension of classroom training.

Finally, an induction program aimed at introducing an employee to his job and moving him ahead in it is more likely to achieve its objectives if there is a convincing rationale underpinning it. Recent experience with adjusting new employees to the job, especially in attempts to curb turnover, have led to a reshaping of ideas about induction. Such reshaping, as reflected in activities before, during, and after hiring, is discussed below.

BEFORE AND DURING HIRING

Preemployment and employment activities should be viewed largely as a decision-making process. Employers have held this view historically, but they have been occupied primarily with their own decision making (deciding whether to hire) rather than with decision making on the part of the applicant (deciding whether to be hired).

Strengthening the applicant's decision making appears to be crucial in fitting new employees comfortably and productively into the job. We should do our best to ensure that the decision to be hired is soundly based on a realistic appraisal of what the applicant is getting into and what is in it for him. If the applicant has such a realistic view and then decides, after weighing the advantages and disadvantages, to accept employment, he is arriving at a job decision by mature judgment rather than momentary impulse. The decision carries a built-in element of commitment.

Equating the "processing" of an applicant with inducting him often results in perfunctory gestures at imparting information—and provides an unreliable basis for the applicant's decision. Only by talking to him about the job, showing him the job, and objectively stating what the job involves, good and bad alike, can the supervisor provide him with the information necessary for a mature decision. If the applicant is too naive to make a decision on his own with such information, the supervisor should attempt to initiate the process by suggesting that he consult his feelings—likes versus dislikes, and so on. In summary, the supervisor should assist the applicant in identifying and weighing the pros and cons.

This approach argues for a longer prehiring period than has been true in the past and a more intensive effort. The supervisor should tell the applicant something about the company and product but should concentrate on the following:

1. The job tasks and surrounding conditions. The supervisor should refer the applicant to the job instructor, if there is one, for some of this information and, more important, for demonstrations.

2. How we will help him master the job, with emphasis on training arrangements and consultations on progress and performance. Training efforts should be nurturing and supportive as well as evaluative, and the applicant should be made to see them in this light.

3. What difficulties or irritations he is likely to run into, with emphasis on any uncontrollable and unpredictable aspects of keeping up the job.

4. What the job has to offer in the way of pay, benefits, steady work, promotional possibilities, and other rewards or satisfactions. A connection should be made between these rewards and such "proper" performance as learning the job, running it efficiently, and coming to work regularly. In addition, an attempt should be made to discover the satisfactions that the applicant is seeking in

the job. Obviously, if his level of aspiration is too high—if he is interested in something we do not have to offer—he is a poor job risk. We would be unwise to hire him, and he will probably eliminate himself.

Even if an applicant accepts the job as a result of these preemployment steps, we would be naive to assume that the commitment is a long-lasting one. However, we can reasonably expect that he will make a genuine effort to learn the job. After employment, we must see to it that the employee's experience actually confirms his commitment rather than raising doubts about it.

The early phase of hiring usually includes giving information as the applicant is "signed up" for employment. A checklist is useful, but problems can arise in the transmission of information. A poorly trained clerk with superficial knowledge and a primary interest in herding people through the process can easily erase the favorable view created by preemployment efforts.

Emphasis should be given to those items of information of immediate concern to the new employee—payroll deductions, enrollment procedures for health and life insurance plans, and other administrative matters. But the basic information on items like pay level and benefit amounts which represent job rewards or satisfactions should already have been given in the preemployment process. Such items can receive expanded coverage during hiring.

AFTER HIRING

After the employee has been hired an effort should be made to confirm his decision and thus strengthen his commitment. The supervisor plays a major role in this process.

Group meetings of new employees, conducted by staff or higher line management, can be held to discuss the broader matters of quality policy, rules of conduct, methods of setting rates and workloads, and similar data pertinent to all jobs. The value of such meetings will be enhanced if they are conducted as interchanges— that is, in terms of what we expect of the employee and what he can expect of us. In addition, role playing can be used during the sessions to foster an understanding of rules of conduct and to build a favorable attitude toward compliance. For example, the new employee, cast in the role of supervisor, can more readily appreciate the dislocations caused by absenteeism and may be more favorably disposed to steady attendance.

The most important aspects of posthiring induction are (1) reviewing job progress and (2) updating expectations of both supervisors and employees as progress mounts. Periodic reviews should be held to examine the current level of performance and current obstacles if any. The reviews should also look ahead to expected accomplishments and to additional or heightened job performance requirements, addressing the emerging or predictable concerns of the new employee as his experience increases and his skill evolves. As he moves toward competency, the employee should be kept continuously aware of what progress is expected of him, and what he can expect, so that the contingency between rewards and performance is firmly retained.

The new employee urgently needs to establish satisfactory working relationships early in the job. The supervisor can make introductions to get the relationships started, but the process will be greatly aided if an instructor is assigned to the employee. The instructor can serve as a sort of sponsor to help the newcomer settle into the relationships and the physical environment; as a source of information and counseling in job-related problems; as a teacher, of course, of job skills; and as a realistic but encouraging shaper of the trainee's job expectations. The instructor should be concerned not only with teaching performance skills but with imparting a knowledge of, a tolerance for, and an ability to cope with the temporary conditions that make the job hard to run. In many jobs such learning is essential to employee persistence. Most important, perhaps, the instructor can serve as a model of an employee who has "made it" and has found satisfaction in the job. It may be useful to expose the new employee to still other employees who have mastered the job and are pleased with the returns.

As is evident from this account, posthiring induction focuses on mastery of the job, as a supplement to direct training efforts. Such mastery is the source of many satisfactions necessary for long-term adjustment to the job. To delay or sidetrack the move toward competency for an encyclopedic infusion of information is a self-defeating venture.

CHAPTER 3

The Vehicular Subjects

THE VEHICULAR SUBJECTS include problem solving, decision making, interviewing, and job organization. These subjects require extensive treatment, since they are universally useful to industrial supervisors in carrying out the substantive activities discussed earlier. Because substantive topics relate to procedures and systems in an individual company, training materials must be developed largely within the company—both the factual material, which details the procedures, and the "action" material, or cases for discussion and role playing that give the supervisor practice in applying procedures before using them on the job itself. By contrast, vehicular subjects deal largely with underlying processes not connected to a specific company, except for some aspects of job organization. Thus outside commercial materials, if carefully chosen, can be useful.

Whenever an activity involves an interchange with employees, as a great many supervisory activities do, interviewing skills are essential. And when procedures strike a snag—when no specific rule or clause or established course of action covers the case—the supervisor must be skilled enough to size up the situation and decide what to do. Problems arise in all realms of the supervisor's functions: quality, efficiency, safety, employee performance, and so on. Of course, skill in carrying out activities is useless if the supervisor does not apply it when the need is present. Training in job organization, as a vehicular subject, is intended to help the supervisor structure the job so as to encompass all its demands and respond to them at appropriate times. Since many events on the job are highly unpredictable, the supervisor's only hope of addressing them and maintaining control lies in systematically scheduling the routine, repetitive activities and allowing sufficient free time to meet unusual contingencies.

Problem Solving

Let us begin the discussion of problem solving by making a distinction, perhaps somewhat artificial, between problems that arise from physical causes (such as machine malfunctioning) and problems that are closely associated with some aspect of employee performance. It is simplistic to say that some problems concern things and some concern people, since contributing factors are often involved. But such a dichotomy is useful in characterizing main issues and in designing appropriate problem-solving approaches or models. If the problem is largely impersonal in nature, having to do with machinery or materials, a "logical analysis" approach to uncovering causes is indicated. When the problem is evidenced by deficiencies in job performance, another problem-solving model will serve, one centering on personal and individual factors that hamper performance.

Whatever the nature of the problem, the pertinent problem-solving procedure contains no magic. It will work well in some cases and only roughly in others. Indeed, the approach may not work at all in some instances; it may not really fit those perverse situations which do not arise by any logical sequence of events. Even when the approach has merit, it may not work for certain people—specifically, for those people whose thinking is not logical.

While supervisors can be taught problem-solving and decision-making procedures, it is often difficult to give them the intellectual framework they need, at the outset, to detect the presence of a problem. Unless the supervisor avoids putting stock in dramatic examples, small deviations, and unreliable or invalid data, he will be chasing will-o'-the-wisps. His earlier education and training, we trust, will have taught him restraint; if not, it may be beyond our power to inculcate it at this late date.

The analysis of evidence also calls for a perceptiveness that may be hard to impart to the new supervisor. Skill in grasping relationships and differences, which give the data meaning, appears to be teachable in part (since perception is related to experience and training), but it also depends on basic intellectual insights that the new supervisor must come equipped to apply.

Indeed, our success in teaching new supervisors to solve problems through application of a procedure is somewhat dependent on a prerequisite ability, however acquired by the supervisors, to avoid an imposing number of semantic and logical fallacies:

1. Projecting their own meaning into words; assuming that the speaker and the hearer are understanding the same things.
2. Assuming that they know everything about a subject that needs to be known; making or accepting unqualified assertions; taking a rigid position that rejects new evidence.
3. Jumping to conclusions on inference; not distinguishing between fact and inference or probability; making false generalizations.
4. Not distinguishing between the relevant and the irrelevant.
5. Taking for granted a conclusion or part of a conclusion that remains to be proved and building a case on it.
6. Using false analogies; seeing a sameness in situations that are different; conversely, treating all situations as new and unprecedented.
7. Assuming that a statistical relationship is a causal relationship.
8. Attributing too heavy an influence (or an absolute or compelling influence) to partial causes; failing to recognize the complexity of causation.

9. Failing to take into account the role of chance in the fluctuation of operational indexes; assuming that action is needed or an instituted action is having an effect on the basis of statistically insignificant variations in the index.

10. Ignoring the past; failing to ascertain tendencies already set in motion by other influences.

DETERMINING THAT A PROBLEM EXISTS

A supervisory problem, simply defined, is a level of operation or performance that is below expectations or standard requirements. If objective measurements and standards are available, an outcome significantly below standard can be validly regarded as a problem. The critical consideration is the extent of the deviation. Since all indexes will fluctuate to some extent through chance alone, small deviations should not stir a supervisor to action. In such cases there is nothing to attack, since no one can control chance. But when the discrepancy is significant (even without the aid of statistics, supervisors can make good judgments on this point) and when it is more than a momentary occurrence, supervisors can be assured that there is something to work on: a genuine problem with causative factors.

If numerical indexes and standards are not available, it is more difficult to detect the presence of a real problem. If incidents are the sole evidence, supervisors must be certain that they constitute a significant deficiency rather than being merely isolated or dramatic examples.

"LOGICAL" PROBLEM SOLVING

There is no mystery about the process of definition which "logical" problem solving basically consists of.* The more precisely we define a problem, the nearer we approach a solution. In effect, if we carry our definition far enough, the cause is likely to stand revealed. This is especially true if the cause is related to a single, identifiable

---

* An early and now widely used model for solving problems that are traceable to changes occurring at a time and place is given in Charles H. Kepner and Benjamin B. Tregoe, *The Rational Manager* (New York: McGraw-Hill Book Company, 1965). A similar model is described in Dugan Laird and Richard Grote, *Solving Management Problems* (Reading, Mass.: Addison-Wesley Publishing Company, 1971).

change or event and is associated with a certain time or place. Problems that arise cumulatively, and from multiple and interrelated causes, are more difficult to dig through; but for the simpler problem a logical process of stating the specifics often serves admirably to provide an answer. Problem definition should focus on the following questions:

What is the deviation? What is its extent?

What and whom does it involve?

When did the difficulty (symptoms) first appear? At what time of day or week are difficulties evident?

Where does the problem arise (in which production areas, work stations, and so on)?

By considering these questions and related distinctions (where not, when not, and so forth), we can often uncover the cause of the current difficulty.

To illustrate, here is a case involving John Henry, a supervisor in a towel mill. The mill was faced with a significant increase in defective finished towels. After examining the inspection records, Henry made a more specific statement of the situation: the percentages of various types of defects had remained relatively constant except for the category "stains and spots," which had experienced a significant increase. Henry requested reinspection of an adequate sample of finished towels and found that the commonest defect in the "stains and spots" classification was "small brown spots" and that these spots were appearing along the hem.

To pin down the "where," Henry examined the product before and after various processes, with special attention to sewing, since the location of the defect along the hemline pointed to sewing as a likely source. Henry reasoned, however, that these defects were not occurring at all sewing stations; otherwise the total mill production of defects would be much higher than it actually was.

After looking at other processes with negative results, Henry attempted to determine, more specifically, at which sewing stations the defects might be originating. Did the stations differ in any way in materials, supplies, operator methods, machines, cleanliness, and so forth? Early in his observation, as he pursued this question,

Henry noted a difference in a minor supply item that justified immediate checking out. The difference was in the "sticky" substance that the hemmers placed on their fingers in order to pick up labels, one at a time, from the container and then position them for sewing on the towel in the hemming cycle.

Henry found that at most sewing stations the hemmers were using a glycerin compound, as specified by the Quality Control Department. But at a number of other stations, the hemmers were using pickle brine brought from home! When these hemmers were asked when they began to use the home substance, they gave an approximate date that corresponded pretty closely with the first appearance, in the records, of an increase in defective towels. An enterprising hemmer had resorted to the home product when the supply of glycerin temporarily ran out, and the practice had spread to a number of other hemmers. Some of them continued to use the product even after the glycerin supply was replenished. Henry further pinned down the "when" by ascertaining from the records that the spots indeed began to appear at about the time the glycerin ran out.

Henry's confirming investigation—tracing the effect of each substance on the finished towel (the defect did not show up until a later finishing process)—revealed the pickle brine to be truly the villain. The hemmers who used the pickle brine, touching the towel along the hem as they applied the label, left undetected spots that "bloomed" later in the finishing operation. No staining occurred with the towels sewn by hemmers who used glycerin.

SHORTCUTTING THE PROCESS

If supervisors have expert knowledge of the manufacturing operations, they can shortcut the problem-solving process. An expert can often zero in on a cause by answering this question: "If I wanted to create this problem, to produce these symptoms, what would I do?" In a real sense, supervisors who have learned well from experience with manufacturing processes have an extensive inventory of cause-and-effect associations for deriving solutions. They dredge up the most appropriate association when a problem arises. But they must confirm the suspected cause. Their expertness informs them that such-and-such an event must have occurred at a certain time or place. Confirmation consists in determining that it has.

This foreshortened approach, providing for a quick movement to possible causes, argues for early development of supervisory proficiency in the technical aspects of manufacturing. If the supervisor has a thorough knowledge (1) of the characteristics and working properties of materials being processed and the effect on the product of materials and supplies used in processing, and (2) of machine operation and maintenance (specifically, the effects of various malfunctions), he can move rather directly to potential causes from symptoms or evidences of technical problems. When he then raises the question, "What would I do if I wanted to create these symptoms?" he has the background for coming to a quick answer. But confirmation is still required, especially when informed inferences are used. All answers, even the answers of acknowledged experts, are inconclusive until confirmed. Did the thing he would do to produce the problem actually occur? If so, he is on sure ground; his inference has become fact.

FACING THE "LARGER" PROBLEMS

Problems that have multiple causes and that develop cumulatively are much harder to handle than problems that can be traced to one specific change at a definite time and place. Unfortunately, in matters of quality and efficiency, the larger problems are likely to be the main ones the supervisor will face.

In confronting such problems, the supervisor must first consider the possibility of multiple and perhaps interrelated causes and take into account the evolving nature of problems. Second, he must deal with the probabilities and uncertainties that accompany such problems. When causes are diagnosed largely through inference, and unavoidably so, the burden of proof resides primarily in the outcome of actions taken to improve the situation. Monitoring, therefore, takes on crucial importance. The supervisor should monitor interim results closely and frequently, keep open an avenue of retreat if the signs are wrong, and be prepared to launch a new course. The danger lies in being locked into a misdirected action through sheer momentum. When a supervisor acts on probabilities, he must realize that he is indeed dealing with probabilities, not certainties, and must leave himself room to maneuver.

Third, the supervisor must reconcile himself to limitations in solving the big problems. If the causes of the problem act independently and cannot be associated with specific changes or discrete events, the supervisor may, at best, be able to confront only one or two legitimate factors, with the modest effect of ameliorating rather than substantially improving the condition but still reducing the problem to tolerable size. To do even this much, he will have to rely heavily on his and others' expertise to give plausible answers to the question: "What could this situation be the result of?" And, again using informed judgment, he will have to evaluate (1) the likelihood that the situation is connected with the suggested cause, and (2) the amount of influence the supposed cause is exerting. To avoid running off in all directions, and to keep the problem-solving and decision-making processes from becoming hopelessly tangled, the supervisor will have to sort out the individual causes and assign them priorities. Of course, it may be possible to work on more than one cause at a time, but the numbers quickly get out of hand, and, as we shall see later, ascribing results to actions becomes a fuzzy matter. But, again, if the supervisor succeeds in uncovering a valid major cause and takes effective action, he may deflate the problem to manageable size. Of course, close monitoring of the action is required to determine whether he has struck paydirt.

If the supervisor attacks several possible causes which are thought to act independently, it is wise, time permitting, to check them out one at a time, holding other conditions as constant as possible in the process. On occasion, when a problem is out of hand and threatens serious damage, the supervisor will have to throw every reasonable weapon into the breach. In such case he may relieve the condition, but he will learn nothing about specific causes and the relative effects of the actions taken. Thus, if the problem again assumes an ominous size, he will have no recourse but to discharge the whole expensive battery again. This is not problem solving.

Problems with multiple causes that are interrelated are especially difficult to solve. Again, the supervisor must rely on expert knowledge of cause-effect relationships in manufacturing and should expect only modest success. But the search for causes must be broad, addressing the expanded question: "What combination of factors is likely to have such an effect?" If the supervisor's knowledge of manufacturing (materials, machinery, equipment, supplies, processing methods, job conditions) is truly extensive, his answers will produce hypotheses worth exploring.

A source of diagnostic difficulty when conditions interact to create a problem is that often the supervisor is dealing not with conditions in the absolute but with degrees of conditions. At such-and-such a point in the interplay of numerous aspects of atmospheric conditions, materials characteristics, processing technology, and employee practices, trouble will occur. The query becomes: "At what critical degree do each of these conditions combine to create the problem?" Or "At what degree does one condition trigger a catalytic reaction in another?"

In such cases, it may be possible to check out the hypotheses before initiating action if standards exist for the suspected elements and are currently valid. For example, in a quality problem the supervisor may suspect that the basic cause lies in the interaction between an evolving change in atmospheric humidity and an evolving imbalance in chemical or physical properties of certain materials. If legitimate standards are available for both conditions, and both are found to be off-standard, the tentative diagnosis gains credence. But confirmation in many cases is not so easy. For certain conditions, standards may not exist or may be out of date. Indeed, the problem may arise from conditions that are functioning within normally acceptable ranges on the indexes. Such conditions may therefore be erroneously dismissed as possible causes.

When advance confirmation is so troublesome in problems with interrelated causes, the best recourse is to take carefully monitored action on the basis of expert judgment. However, the supervisor will not enjoy the luxury of being able to evaluate one action at a time; he will probably have to resort to actions aimed at the suspected interlocking causes. Further, the resolution of such a problem may not be a return to beginning or earlier states, since some of the evolving conditions may be largely irreversible; instead, a new accommodation of forces may need to be worked out. Finally, additional decisions must be made on the intensity of the actions and how long to pursue them.

A large and complex problem that has evolved slowly over time must be handled with patience. The problem is not likely to disappear tomorrow, no matter how skillfully the supervisor addresses it. If the problem is related to a wide range of operations, specific remedies may not be possible and an overhaul of technical aspects of the operation or of supervisory activities may be required. The supervisor himself may be part of the problem.

Decision Making

Once a supervisor has settled on the cause of a problem, he faces the additional chore, virtually indistinguishable from problem solving, of deciding on a course of action. A useful procedure is to begin by evaluating possible actions to determine if they are reasonable, practical (with regard to resources, for example), and related to the cause being confronted. For each of the actions meeting this preliminary test, the supervisor then considers the possible consequences of taking the action, weighing the good against the bad. In this examination, the likelihood of the anticipated consequences should be taken into account. Obviously, a potentially favorable result that is highly unlikely should carry very little weight. Similarly, a highly improbable negative consequence should be given little stature as a deterrent. The preferred action is the one having the greatest preponderance of possible favorable results over unfavorable. Finally, the supervisor makes specific plans for carrying out the selected course of action, including an advance strategy for confronting foreseeable contingencies.

The decision, of course, must be logically and economically sound, but it also must be capable of execution. And since execution involves people, their acceptance of the decision is a significant consideration—one that we often lose sight of. The sabotaging of supposedly "good" decisions is a recurrent lament among supervisors who act arbitrarily.

If a decision is to be accepted, employees must see it as serving their self-interest or, at least, as not seriously threatening it. Since employees' self-interests differ and often conflict, the supervisor is faced with the task of arriving at the sort of decision that will reconcile these interests. He will be hard put to do this on his own; he is not sure of how people perceive things, and he is even less sure whether accommodation is possible. One workable solution, if the situation is right for participation, is to throw the problem on the table and allow the employees directly involved to reconcile their differences. The decision that emerges usually has the sanction of these employees and, more important, their informal commitment to carry it out with goodwill. The supervisor must make sure, of course, that the decision is economically sound; but to secure acceptance he may have to settle for something less than the economically optimal solution.

CARRYING OUT THE DECISION

The new supervisor must realize that a decision is not self-propelling or self-correcting. Its execution and monitoring must be carefully planned, along with contingency actions for meeting foreseeable difficulties.

Experience is a good basis for planning action and carrying it out, but caution is necessary. Supervisors are wise to repeat an action when a situation recurs in which it was previously successful. However, the new situation is rarely a duplicate of the old. The greater the differences, the less likely the old approach will work. The supervisor's earlier learning, reinforced by past success, will lead to trouble when the new situation is different. A new approach is essential when the new situation is unique and when the course of action requires creativity and experimentation. When faced with an unchartable course, the supervisor must call upon the resources available to him in the larger organization—the experience, expertise, and creative thinking of others—to plan his passage through the maze.

A course of action will involve "who" as well as "what" and "how." Few major decisions can be carried out by one supervisor alone, and their effects are rarely confined to the supervisor's own jurisdiction. Other people inevitably come into the picture, either participating in the action or affected by it. Thus, in the planning stage, the supervisor must prepare participants for the roles they will play, secure acceptance from those who will be directly or indirectly affected, and provide channels of communication to interested "spectators" in the organization.

Advance planning of actions and contingency arrangements does not guarantee skillful execution. In monitoring, the supervisor will know how well things are going, but when difficulties arise, he cannot be sure whether the fault lies in the tactic or in its execution. Was it a poor step to take or a good step poorly done? The supervisor should analyze the causes of difficulties carefully, taking both plan and execution into account. A good action poorly performed is not necessarily invalid. Often the damage can be repaired with improved execution the second time around. But a qualitatively poor step should be discarded, and plans revised accordingly.

Follow-up is obviously essential for evaluating both tactics and performance—whether the action is based on experience or experimentation (though the latter will require closer attention). Frequent monitoring is important, particularly early in the game, since errors tend to gain momentum and their effects to spread quickly. If benchmarks for judging or measuring progress have been established (as they should be), they can serve as points of reference in the evaluation of progress.

When there is substantial unpredictability in the outcome, decision making takes on an experimental character, and the supervisor should think, at least informally, in terms of experimental design. If he decides on a single course of action, he should proceed with it and not embark blindly on other ventures that might affect the objective. He should also try to keep conditions as stable as possible to control the intrusion of other influences. When several courses of action are executed at the same time, complications arise in pinning down the effects of each course. As indicated earlier, if an emergency or near-disaster arises and short-term improvement is called for, the question of relative contributions is academic. The supervisor simply tries to overwhelm the problem by attacking on all fronts. But if he is concerned with efficiency of effort (which he normally must be) and expects to learn something from the experience for future reference, the massive assault will put him at a disadvantage. He does not know exactly what caused the outcome.

Consider the case of Donald Ferguson, a production department supervisor who was faced with an efficiency problem. His exploration of causes led him, correctly, to certain mechanical settings on his machines. The settings had been established as standard several years earlier but had not been changed when adjustments were made in the blend of raw materials and in certain running conditions. Ferguson instructed his repairmen to use new settings that were more appropriate to the changed materials and conditions. In his follow-up he found efficiency falling even more.

After fruitless discussions with his repairmen, Ferguson conducted a new investigation which revealed that at the time he introduced the mechanical changes, the raw material blend had been changed in the Preparation Department (two steps removed from his department's operation). He had not been informed and therefore had not been able to control a major influence on efficiency—the nature of the raw material. As a result, he could not validly evaluate the effect of his course of action.

OPTION REVIEW

Versatility is essential in decision making, since situations differ and solutions cannot all be arrived at with recourse to one rigid procedure. For example, replacement decisions—whether in response to an operational problem or as a separate, self-evident issue—are a continuing requirement. It is a fact of industrial life, as in all of life, that nothing lasts forever. Machinery, equipment, and facilities in general wear out or become obsolete. Supplies are consumed.

To help supervisors meet these varying needs, we should provide them with additional decision-making models, judiciously chosen. There is no point in forcing on them the troublesome chore of deciding among a number of poorly understood models. Of course, they must decide how to decide and must select the procedure most appropriate to the particular case, but they should have a limited though adequate repertoire of well-understood approaches pertinent to their operation.

A useful supplementary approach, designed for selecting the best of a number of alternatives, is the option review. This procedure involves weighing the advantages of the various options against significant factors or criteria. For display and ease of understanding, a matrix format is particularly helpful. In this type of table, the options are shown at the top, with the factors or considerations listed at the side. The body of the matrix includes rankings of the various options, from best to poorest, on each factor. (Parametric values can also be used if they are available or can be estimated with some accuracy.)

To illustrate, let us say that a supervisor had to choose from among three "makes" of machine to replace old machinery in his department. A possible ranking of options is shown in Table 3 (giving, so as to permit later arithmetic manipulation, a value of 3 to the best, 2 to the second best, and 1 to the worst). In this case, the final choice would seem to fall between machine A and machine C, with C given the edge because of its slightly better average rank. However, such a "straight" ranking is misleading in that it overstates (or understates) the relative importance of the individual criteria. A further refinement of the approach—weighting the various factors—brings the rankings into better focus. Operating efficiency and the cost of machines would seem to be more important

TABLE 3.
Option review by ranking.

| Factors | Machine Choices | | |
	A	B	C
Machine cost	2	1	3
Installation cost	2	1	3
Maintenance cost	2	1	3
Processing efficiency (measured hourly output —manufacturer's data)	3	2	1
Total rank	9	5	10
Average rank	2.3	1.3	2.5

TABLE 4.
Option review by weighted ranking.

Factors	Weight	A Rank	A Wted. Rank	B Rank	B Wted. Rank	C Rank	C Wted. Rank
Machine cost	3	2	6	1	3	3	9
Installation cost	1	2	2	1	1	3	3
Maintenance cost	2	2	4	1	2	3	6
Processing efficiency	6	3	18	2	12	1	6
Total weighted rank			30		18		24
Average weighted rank (total divided by number of weights—12)			2.5		1.5		2.0

than installation cost. Further distinctions could be made. For example, using his best judgment on relative importance, the supervisor might give heaviest weight (6) to processing efficiency, second heaviest (3) to cost of machines, third heaviest (2) to maintenance costs, and least weight (1) to installation costs. The matrix would now look like Table 4. The weighting reveals that machine A is clearly the best choice, taking due account of its efficiency of operation.

When actual values or reliable estimates are available, they should be arranged in a matrix for comparison of the relative merits of the options. Such a matrix is shown in Table 5.

Calculations of the various factors (perhaps additional ones, as well) would indicate the profit per unit. Let us assume, in order to complete the illustration, that the gain in profit from machine A would quickly make up for the differences in immediate outlay (machine and installation costs) and offset higher maintenance costs continuously by a comfortable margin.

Whatever method is used for decision making, the decision will be no better than the data used. The sophistication of the technique

TABLE 5.
Option review of parametric values.

Factors	Machine Choices		
	A	B	C
Cost per machine (actual)	$1,000	$1,500	$800
Installation cost per machine (actual)	100	120	75
Maintenance cost per machine (weekly estimate)	155	170	150
Processing efficiency (output per hour per machine)	200 units	190 units	185 units

adds nothing to the reliability of the figures. Early in his training in problem solving and decision making, the new supervisor should be made aware of the gradations in reliability of evidence—from hearsay through memory, statistical evidence, and expert opinion to physical measurements—and of the differences between hard and soft data so that he will not read more into his decisions than the data will support.

FORMALITY OF APPROACH

A pertinent question often asked by supervisors is: How formal should the problem-solving and decision-making process be? The question is usually accompanied by an insistence on practicality in the "real" world of the supervisor.

Only the exceptional supervisor will labor through a detailed analysis of the problem within a strict format or systematically evaluate the relative advantages of possible actions. But by the very nature of his job the supervisor does consider causes of problems and weigh his options. And if it is too much to expect him to conduct a thorough written analysis, we should expect him to proceed rationally in probing for causes, deciding what to do, and organizing the data meaningfully so that he can draw valid conclusions.

Any approach, formal or informal, is worth the training effort required to bring it about. With complex problems, however, we should emphasize the use of visible procedures that conform at least roughly to appropriate models. Otherwise, the supervisor may ignore certain important considerations and the accompanying data or become overwhelmed by a multiplicity of factors and figures. When problems are complex, the data simply have to be set out in a sensible array at the very least. If not, the supervisor is struggling with an incomprehensible mishmash and has little recourse but to rely on a store of pet solutions built up from experience. A new supervisor, with no significant experience, does not even have this "informed intuition" to call upon.

While a systematic approach to problem solving and decision making is highly recommended, a search for absolute answers is not. Aside from the limitations, in terms of time and skills, in making such a quest, the basic question of justification arises. When a solution is found that reasonably fulfills the criteria of authenticity and practicality, the possible gain from seeking a better answer may not justify the prolonged search. Besides, in the supervisor's uncertain world, the ultimate answer is not over the horizon—or anywhere else.

MOVING FROM CONCEPTS TO APPLICATIONS

Skill in problem solving, decision making, and the execution of decisions must be developed—an obvious truth that should inform all our training efforts. We cannot settle for describing a model in the abstract and discussing execution in broad terms with simple review of dos and don'ts, leaving the new supervisor to sink or swim on the job.

To prepare the supervisor adequately, we must go beyond concepts. With nonpersonnel problems, which we have been considering to this point in the chapter, we should present the supervisor with a problem-solving model, by lecture and illustration, to give him a conceptual grasp of the procedure. We then progress to a discussion of increasingly realistic cases in the classroom. These cases should serve as illustrations, not to teach applications to specific kinds of problems. We begin to work on applications by discussing problems related to manufacturing operations. Since the objective at this point is to give the supervisor stronger insight into the procedure, the precise nature of the case problem is not the compelling consideration. Once this objective is met, the procedure can be brought to bear on problems more pertinent to the supervisor's operation. We can present more specific applications by discussing problems in substantive matters such as quality and efficiency. These discussions should be conducted in courses dealing with the particular substantive subjects. The final training effort involves coaching in handling current problems on the job itself.

A similar training procedure applies to decision making. We need to give the new supervisor a clear understanding of the model, practice in applying it to case situations, and eventually coaching in issues that arise on the job itself. In the decision-making course, we present and illustrate the model and discuss cases of various sorts to firm up understanding of the procedure. Then, in courses dealing with substantive matters, we apply the procedure and the supervisor's budding skill in it to operational decisions.

However, classroom case discussion—in the decision-making course itself or in substantive courses—cannot proceed very far into execution of the decision. Simulation simply becomes too difficult to contrive. On the job, the effects of a planned series of steps are not completely predictable; each action sets in motion a unique train of events. To treat execution of a decision, in class, as a static, cut-and-dried process is to disregard reality. And to duplicate reality in class is impossible. So the teaching of execution should be left largely to on-the-job coaching.

What can be taught in class about decision execution is the planning of remedial steps, the exploration of predictable difficulties, and the development of tactics for meeting such contingencies. A useful exercise is to have the supervisor write scenarios that explore the possible consequences of decisions and of steps in their execution. ("What will happen if. . . ?" "What is the worst thing that can happen if. . . ?")

Although coaching in job decisions is highly recommended as a training technique, it must be discriminating. Since seasoned supervisors have a background of experience that permits them to short-cut procedures, the coach must tread a somewhat narrow ground, interjecting his own experience as needed so that difficulties are not compounded but permitting the new supervisor some leeway to explore alternatives. The coach must also allow short-cutting of the procedure as the new supervisor gains knowledge and experience, but he should not permit trial-and-error efforts in place of a logical attack.

The new supervisor will need particular guidance in the "personnel" aspect of putting a decision in motion, since people are the most unpredictable element in the formula.

Performance Problems

If an employee's performance is unsatisfactory or has dropped significantly, the cause is likely to be an inadequacy in one or more of the following: skill, motivation, and job conditions.* Before analyzing these and other factors, the supervisor must again be sure he has a problem. Is the discrepancy so small that the probabilities heavily favor chance as an explanation? Does it represent a momentary aberration, a reaction perhaps to a self-correcting condition that will fade before he can wheel his problem-solving model into action?

If a genuine problem exists, it is useful to proceed through a series of questions related to general factors that can affect performance. These questions should be considered in order—at least, job-related causes should be examined before causes that are personal in nature. And the supervisor should exhaust other possibilities before concluding that the employee is basically incapable of mastering the job. The questions:

1. Does the employee have adequate skill?
2. Is he willing (or "motivated") to perform?

* For a diagnostic approach to performance problems, see Robert F. Mager and Peter Pipe, *Analyzing Performance Problems, Or 'You Really Oughta Wanna'* (Belmont, Cal.: Fearon Publishers, 1970); J. H. Harless, *An Ounce of Analysis (Is Worth a Pound of Objectives)* (McLean, Va.: Harless Performance Guild, 1975); and James E. Gardner, *Helping Employees Develop Job Skill* (Washington, D.C.: The Bureau of National Affairs, 1976), pp. 114–119, 150–154.

3. Can the job really be run well?
4. Are outside or personal matters influencing his performance?
5. Does he have the necessary aptitude for reaching an acceptable level of performance?

SKILL PROBLEMS

The chief means of checking out inadequate skill as a cause is to observe the employee on the job for a long enough time to get a reliable reading, and to observe him thoroughly and analytically so as to detect subtle aspects of performance which a cursory look will not reveal. Such observation provides a running start on the solution, since it helps pinpoint the feature of job execution that is at fault. Inadequate skill will be found to reside in the following:

1. Inefficient job methods.
2. Slowness (not related to effort).
3. Poor organization of the job.
4. Inability to cope with unusual, but controllable, job conditions.

In carrying the diagnosis this far, the supervisor will at least avoid humiliating the experienced employee by making an unwarranted attempt to retrain him in the total job. But, as touched upon earlier in the discussion of skills training, the precision of the remedy will depend on a finer-grained diagnosis that identifies the causes of general difficulties in skill.

If job methods are at fault, is it simply a matter of excessive motions serving no purpose? Or is the employee purposefully using wrong motions to compensate for poor execution in some other part of the task cycle? Is the poor motion pattern, then, the employee's own uninformed solution to his problem, permitting him at least to complete the task? In eliminating purposeless motions, the supervisor can concentrate on the motions themselves as the problem. In eliminating purposeful motions, the supervisor must find out precisely what the employee is doing to make such motions necessary. The cause of the problem lies not in the compensating motions but in what calls them forth.

If the difficulty is tied to inadequate speed in executing the task, even when the employee expends strong effort, analysis will probably reveal that the fault lies not in motions but in inefficient feedback. The employee is taking too much time to check where he stands along the way because he is referring to unnecessary checkpoints or is using a less efficient sensory channel in his perception (vision rather than the kinesthetic sense, for example). Or—again related to perceptual difficulties—he may be held up in the transition between subtasks, holding excessively long to feedback from the first and failing to anticipate the next. Or he may be performing subtasks consecutively when they should be done simultaneously, most likely because he is relying on the same sensory channel for feedback from both.

If the employee is having trouble with organizing the job, the supervisor needs to ask such questions as these: In which tasks does the employee's planning fall short? What is he failing to do or failing to do on time? What are his priorities when two or more job demands occur at the same time? Which tasks, already undertaken, does he abandon when other tasks demand attention? At what point in their execution does he leave one task for another?

If the employee is having trouble coping with an unusual job condition, the supervisor needs to identify the difficulty. Does it involve the mechanical condition of machines, the condition of materials, environmental variables, the way the job is left by the preceding shift—or what? Once the burdensome condition is revealed, it should be dissected further to determine the exact nature of the employee's efforts to cope with it and the shortcomings of such efforts. Does he recognize the need for action? What actions does he take? What adjustments does he make—in the planning, scheduling, and organization of his activities—to confront the condition?

MOTIVATION PROBLEMS

A tip-off that motivation may be the general problem is skilled performance in combination with a poor record of output. When observed, the employee executes job tasks competently and keeps the job under control, but his output over a period of days or weeks falls substantially below standard. In addition, absenteeism may be high. In short, the employee is not applying himself persistently to the job, indicating that motivation is at fault.

The means of providing motivation are not easy to come by. The usual conclusion is that good performance is not being reinforced or sufficiently reinforced. And the usual prescription is to provide such reinforcement, using whatever rewards are available and making them clearly contingent on good performance. Possible reinforcers range from expressions of supervisory approval to minor tangible rewards in the way of treats, gifts, and privileges, to major rewards such as pay increases and promotions. The supervisor must not believe, however, that simply using reinforcers will sustain the employee's performance. As we will see later, the sustaining of performance through reinforcers appears to depend on such factors as level of aspiration, satiety, and the function of the reward as an instrumental means of achieving higher satisfactions. Ultimately, self-reinforcement apparently must provide the propelling force.

In large part, these are highly personal issues which are not well known and over which even competent supervisors can expect to exert only limited influence. The primary help we can give supervisors is to teach them to maximize rewards within their control and to communicate clearly so that employees have a realistic understanding of the rewards available through good performance.

MANAGEABILITY OF THE JOB

The major clue that the manageability of the job is the obstacle to good performance is the scope of the problem: the job is operated satisfactorily by no other employee or by very few; or there is a history of poor performance among employees on the job. A related indication is a high turnover rate, since most employees will not persist in a losing battle unless counterpressures are strong. If they do persist, they are likely to react with aggression, rigidity, childishness, and other signs of frustration.

On such jobs, waiting time and repair time tend to be heavy, and the flow of materials may be uneven. Another element—unpredictability—adds to the employee's frustration. The machinery may fail at unforeseen times, the processing characteristics of the material may change unexpectedly, or atmospheric conditions may be subject to capricious shifts.

Unless job activities are highly regular, offering the possibility of "encompassing" the job, with no loose ends or surprises outside their control, many employees will find that they cannot function effectively and will eventually write off the job as impossible to perform—even if they remain in it.

When poor performance, as measured by the usual indexes, is related to the basic nature of the job or its uncontrollable features, the supervisor's only recourse is to make the job as manageable as possible. His attack should be discriminating, focusing on specific factors that prevent adequate performance—such as machinery, equipment, materials, and surrounding conditions. Although the supervisor is not in a position to reengineer the job himself, he can make recommendations to his line superior and staff engineers. And he may be able to take minor action on his own to ameliorate the problem, making possible a significant improvement in the employee's performance.

PERSONAL PROBLEMS

Personal problems, as a cause of poor performance, are often signaled by a relatively swift change in behavior. The good and reliable employee one day becomes inattentive and commits oversights; his preoccupation with his own dilemma shows up in a drop in output or quality and perhaps in a higher susceptibility to accidents.

These periods of stress and the accompanying slippage in performance are not likely to last long, but the new supervisor must be able to spot the observable symptoms and should take whatever action he can to ease the employee through the crisis. His actions will be limited. But simply serving as a sympathetic listener and a source of referral may prove helpful to the employee. The supervisor should not make the mistake of pressuring the distressed employee for better performance and thus compounding the employee's troubles and perhaps producing further deterioration in performance.

There has been a running dispute for years on whether the

supervisor has a proper function as a counselor. Although the relationship between supervisor and employee may be more open now than in the past, the conventional wisdom is to circumscribe the supervisor's effort to help employees with personal problems. Experience still seems to give strong support to a restrained approach.

If job performance suffers because of personal problems, the supervisor can legitimately discuss the matter with the employee. However, inquiries should be circumspect and not aimed at trapping the employee into making involuntary disclosures. When there are no manifestations on the job, the employee's personal problems are a private matter not subject to the supervisor's scrutiny.

Within these rather narrow bounds, the supervisor can have some effect, but primarily in helping the employee resolve his own difficulties rather than in giving counsel. The following guidelines are helpful in playing this role:

1. Listen patiently, sympathetically, and understandingly. Remain objective; neither condemn nor condone questionable conduct.
2. Let the employee do the talking. Restate his position or expression of feeling now and again, but avoid misinterpretation.
3. Listen long enough to permit the employee to pass beyond emotions to the point where he can examine his problem more objectively.
4. Answer questions of fact but do not voice personal opinions.
5. Do not give advice. The effect on the continuing relationship can be disastrous.
6. Refer the employee to sources of professional help, either in the organization or in the community.
7. Keep quiet after the discussions; do not betray the employee's confidence.

LACK OF SUITABILITY FOR THE JOB

Only after looking carefully at the other factors and validly rejecting them can the supervisor conclude that the employee is not suited to the particular job. An inexperienced supervisor is likely to reach such a conclusion prematurely. It is the easy way out, often serving as an excuse for failing to give adequate training generally or to take into account the employee's unique training needs. The supervisor may throw the employee into the job to sink or swim with very little help and then conclude, when he predictably sinks, that he was not cut out for the job after all.

When a standard training procedure is used and the employee fails to respond, the supervisor may erroneously place the blame on "unsuitability for the job." What may really be unsuitable is the training approach—if it is not geared to the individual's training needs or adaptable to his stage of development. Only when a truly insightful and flexible training approach, with pertinent teaching techniques, fails to produce results should the question of employee suitability be raised. Still, the question cannot be fully resolved until the factors of motivation, job manageability, and personal problems have been eliminated.

MULTIPLE AND INTERRELATED CAUSES

Multiple causes are sometimes at play in poor performance, and they often feed on one another. Poor or misdirected training can produce a loss of motivation, which in turn undermines learning. An unmanageable job will reduce motivation and defy training.

If analysis of job performance uncovers evidence of multiple, interlocking difficulties, it is essential to attack the basic one. It is fruitless to work on training or motivation if the job, no matter how skillfully and enthusiastically undertaken, will not run. If, with the supervisor's help, the employee is able to bring the job under control, other factors may clear up with little attention from the supervisor.

As a rule of thumb, when symptoms of poor learning and low motivation appear together, learning should be attacked first. It is difficult, in any event, to work on motivation strictly in itself. If the supervisor focuses on a better training approach, with reinforcement of improved performance as a major feature, we can perhaps move the skill forward in a way intrinsically satisfying to the employee and provide him with the highly motivating experience of success. In such a case, as learning improves, motivation may improve.

SUPERVISORY TRAINING IN IMPROVING EMPLOYEE JOB PERFORMANCE

The supervisor cannot proceed very far in analyzing or correcting poor performance without talking directly to the employee. The employee's input is a necessary ingredient in both, since his performance is involved. He is directly confronted with the difficulty and in most cases (except for job conditions) must be the instrument of improvement. This is not to say that he has insight, though he may, into the cause of his problem or into possible remedies; but he is painfully aware of the general nature of his difficulty. And with skillful probing, the supervisor may uncover the specific cause, so that both employee and supervisor are prepared to address it.

The kind of interview useful for analyzing performance difficulties and deciding on a course of action should not be a minimal interchange, with a resultant haphazard jumping to conclusions. Rather, the interview should proceed logically from a review of the evidence of the problem through a discussion of causes to a decision on what to do and how to monitor the doing. Such an interview was outlined earlier in connection with learning difficulties; it is equally useful in analyzing performance problems arising from any other source. Of course, the problem cannot be resolved solely through interviews, but such contacts with the employee, along with observations, are a major part of the process.

The foundation for developing supervisory skill in such interviews can be laid in a general interviewing course, with attention to eliciting information—a basic procedure in the search for causes of poor performance.

In the full scope of his training in the handling of performance problems, the new supervisor can be given knowledge, through explanation and illustration in class sessions, of factors influencing job performance and can become familiar with the signs (with emphasis on objective evidence) of poor performance. In such sessions, he can also acquire some measure of skill in analyzing performance problems and conducting interviews through realistic cases for discussion and role playing. As stated earlier, background training in interview models is useful. Coaching on the job is the critical final training arrangement. Skill can be developed quickly through guided handling of performance problems on the job itself, because the experience will pile up in a hurry as the supervisor is faced with an almost uninterrupted procession of problems.

PERFORMANCE OF SYSTEMS

Supervisors are concerned not only with the performance of individual employees but with the larger issue of the performance of the system—that combination of employees and machinery that is, in effect, the enterprise. The level of performance achieved by the elements in the system, and the success of the interactions among them, will depend on whether their full potential has been realized. Are the people and things, singly and in combination, functioning optimally?

One evidence of high performance is objective results—as represented, for example, by output or efficiency figures. But the supervisor cannot judge the performance of the system by results alone. Certainly, he cannot assume that the system is in good health simply because the figures on the major index are good. The process should also be taken into account. Output can be raised temporarily by neglecting maintenance, quality, and safety—simply by keeping the machines running, with patchwork measures, beyond the recommended limits of speed or durability, until they "fall on the floor."

Keeping in mind both results and process, we might describe a high-performance system in a production department as one in which, in normal circumstances, the machinery runs smoothly, the raw material is highly workable, no bottlenecks occur in the flow of material or delivery of supplies, surrounding conditions are favorable, and individual employees (machine operators, repairmen, and materials handlers) are skilled in their jobs and work with timely and effective coordination.

To say that an operation is "under control" does not fully describe a high-performance operation. Rather, it clicks; it hums. The elements are under rein but are given their head, so to speak. They move.

An operation will not enjoy normal conditions indefinitely, and it is another mark of the high-performance production system that it efficiently confronts unforeseen, uncontrollable events. Modification in production specifications, installation of updated machinery, introduction of raw materials with different processing properties, and changes in surrounding conditions are examples of such events. The high-performance system takes these events in stride; it has the will, expertise, ingenuity, and adaptability to absorb the new requirements quickly and work them into its operating routine. In a good unit there may be gripes about how "they're always changing things," but the response is a rather direct and positive attack on the problem. This is true for temporary emergencies as well as long-lasting changes in operation.

High activity is not synonymous with high performance, and frenetic activity is almost certainly not a sign of high performance. In a high-performance weave room, for example, it is amazing how little activity is evident to the casual observer. Weavers appear to be leisurely strolling among the looms or passing the time of day with loomfixers. A loomfixer stands idly at his workbench. Little work is going on at the looms themselves; here and there a weaver is drawing in an end or a fixer is making a repair or a warp crew is replacing a loom beam.

But the system is running in high gear and producing. The strolling weavers are patrolling their looms to spot potential yarn breaks and to detect the first signs of fabric defects. Their conversations with fixers have to do with the conditions of certain looms, the scores of conference games, the condition of warps, the way the fish are biting at Philpott, the quality of the cloth. The looms in the idle loomfixer's section are all banging away and making good cloth. When the looms need direct attention, they get it without delay. The ends are drawn in skillfully and swiftly by the weavers; the warp beams are replaced—a heavy and intricate process—by special crews with deft coordination and a parsimony of motions. The looms are soon back in production.

It all appears rather casual to the outsider, and it is the despair of those industrial engineers who like to see employees' hands actively occupied at all times. But everything becomes strikingly purposeful when understood; the seemingly idle or aimless behaviors are preventive measures to reduce the necessity for labor, and the active behaviors are a swift and sure response when the necessity occurs. It works.

If the supervisor is to aid in the development of high-performance systems, there are certain characteristics or qualifications he must possess and certain acts he must perform. First of all, he should be well versed in the technology of the operation and in its special vocabulary. Moreover, he should be able to recognize a high-performance system and understand its criteria of performance. If such criteria are opposed to departmental objectives (an overemphasis on quality at the expense of output, for example), he will have to intervene. His understanding of the system will give him guidance on actions he should take to reestablish criteria and, more important, to reorient and possibly reshape the processes by which criteria are met. With these characteristics, the supervisor is more likely to be an active participant in the system—perhaps its leader in fact as well as position—rather than a spectator who makes demands on the system.

There are a number of things the supervisor can do to build or strengthen the system. As best he can, he should select employees who appear to have an interest in the kind of activity the operation requires. He should then do a thorough job of training so that the new employee is in a position to contribute appreciable skill to the operation rather than exerting a drag on it.

Whether a new employee is accepted by the established members of a high-performance system will depend largely on whether he likes what the system does and whether he is any good at it. New employees who are, in effect, transients, unwilling to commit themselves to learning the job or to make an effort to run it, are unwelcome in high-performance systems. Indeed, they affront the system.

In monitoring job methods, the supervisor should watch for inefficient methods rather than simply for deviations from the standard. A common practice in establishing a standard method in a manipulative job is to fit motions with predetermined time values on an observed variety of methods and then select the method whose cumulative motions take the least time. The resulting rather mechanistic methods statement may serve to introduce a novice to the task, but it will often be modified by the employee as he acquires skill. Performance feedback, particularly the evolving reliance of kinesthetic cues (the "feel" of the motion) by employees as experience mounts, often leads to subtle shortcuts in method. In addition, the experienced employee may experiment with a method that is substantially different from the standard in motion pattern and sequence of steps.

The supervisor should allow skilled employees a certain amount of invention, by drawing the line at inefficient methods but accepting equivalent methods and embracing superior ones. There is really no way to stop experimentation in a high-performance system; employees will inevitably seek a better way.

Jobs should be kept as manageable as possible. Although a high-performance system will overcome difficulties better than a low-performance system, even the best of systems is unlikely to withstand a constant barrage of problems. It will absorb them, but at spaced intervals to allow the restructuring process to run its course. The system must have time to settle into a groove, to develop smoothness and precision in its ongoing operations.*

Interviewing

Initial training in interviewing should deal with the basic communications difficulties that beset all our efforts to exchange meaning with one another by word of mouth, no matter what the content or the purpose of the exchange.† Chief among these difficulties are the tendency to make statements of inference rather than fact and the tendency to project one's own meaning into the other person's words or message. New supervisors should be instructed in how

* Peter Vaill has been in the forefront of inquirers into the characteristics of high-performance systems. His presentation, "Understanding High-Performance Systems," given at the 1978 National Conference of the American Society for Training and Development, has been made available on audio cassette tape by ASTD, Madison, Wisconsin.

† For an entertaining and astute treatment of communication difficulties, with emphasis on semantics, and practical pointers for overcoming them, see Irving J. Lee and Laura L. Lee, *Handling Barriers in Communication* (New York: Harper & Brothers, 1957).

these and similar mechanisms work, with emphasis on how the misunderstandings they produce can lead to erroneous acts. It is the effect on the employee's acts—and the supervisor's as well—which makes the interchange so important.

Successful oral communication is primarily a matter of securing enough playback from the employee, through judicious use of questions, to ensure that the message gets through and that it carries the same meaning for the supervisor and the employee. The questions should go far enough to achieve clarification but should not be offensive or demeaning to the employee. And since communication is a two-way process, with possible misinterpretation by either party, the supervisor should also make sure that he understands the employee's responses. This objective requires that the supervisor ask pertinent questions and hear the employee out.

Classroom role-playing exercises can give the new supervisor early practice in transmitting information. At this point, the subject of the message is not as important as the process of clarification, so any relatively realistic material will serve—for example, induction information on conditions of employment, information on job hazards, and information on disciplinary policy.

In the role-playing exercises, the supervisor should be given guidelines, with advance explanation and discussion, that will serve as a procedure to be mastered by him and as points of reference for gauging the effectiveness of his role-playing interviews. For example:

Guidelines for Transmitting Information

1. Be ready in advance. Have all the information available; have it organized in a logical framework or outline; and have illustrations and examples at hand.
2. Make the start a meaningful one. Explain the purpose of the interview; take account of what the listener already knows but do not make assumptions about his knowledge or perceptions.
3. Give an organized presentation:
   —Present the points in logcial order.
   —Use pertinent illustrations and examples; use multiple media if practical.

—Use repetition.

—Help the listener identify the most important points—by emphasis, repetition, and placement in the list (get back to them at the *end*).

—Give *all* the needed information.

—Give an overview to sum things up and further emphasize key points.

4. Pace the interview to give the listener time to absorb the information. Go slow on the major points.

5. Check for understanding—along the way, so that misunderstanding does not pile up, and again at the end. Get playback—answers to specific questions of content.

Interchanges with employees are also intended to elicit information. Again, role-playing exercises will serve (although the process rather than the content is the primary consideration). The supervisor should be guided by a set of principles, such as those listed below:

Guidelines for Eliciting Information

1. Ask questions in a simple and straightforward way, in terms the respondent understands.

2. Ask questions that require full responses, rather than "yes" or "no" (except when seeking confirmation of an answer). Use words like "when," "where," "what," "why," and "how."

3. Give the employee an opportunity to answer. Do not intervene too early with another question, argue with the respondent, or offer what you think is his answer before hearing him out.

4. Encourage him to continue once he has begun to talk, using such nondirective methods as these:

—Simple acknowledgment of what he has said ("I see," "Yes").

—Restatement of what he has said. (Avoid misstatement.)

—Restatement of how he feels on the subject. (Avoid misinterpretation.)

5. Allow latitude in the discussion. If the respondent goes far astray, bring him back to the subject without offending. But

do not decide prematurely that the respondent is not speaking to the point; he may have an "angle" you never thought of.
6. Keep an open mind and show a genuine interest in hearing him out.

Another general purpose of interchanges is to convince or persuade other people of one's point of view. As with the other functions discussed above, the supervisor should be given instruction in the procedural steps of conducting this type of interview and practice through role playing. Again, any reasonably realistic cases may be used, since the early emphasis is not on specific situations in which employees must be convinced or employee attitudes changed but on the interview process itself. Here are some procedural pointers:

Guidelines for Making a Convincing Case

1. Make sure you understand the idea or action fully.
2. Make sure that you yourself are convinced that the idea or action is a good one.
3. Do not assume that the respondent will agree to the wisdom of the idea or action simply on your say-so. Make a full case for it.
4. Present the points in your case in logical order and use words the respondent understands.
5. Emphasize the advantages of the idea, if any, to the respondent. But do not overstate them.
6. If the idea or action poses any disadvantages, temporary or otherwise, discuss them fully. Do not ignore or gloss over them.
7. If the course of action is not already fixed and the situation is right for participation, allow the respondent to present his point of view.

Since it is so difficult to counter unfavorable attitudes with information, the supervisor could use supplementary pointers in this undertaking, along with expanded opportunity for practice. First of all, he should take a modest stance; he should realize that it is unrealistic to expect a radical shift in attitude and should keep in mind that he is not the only source of information and influence. He should also be aware that the amount of information he possesses and the way he presents it will affect the outcome of the interview. If he is not really knowledgeable in the subject—or is not seen as expert by the respondent—his influence will be undercut. He should present the information in a straightforward and unbiased manner, without trying to "snow" or "hardsell" the employee. This is not to rule out an emphasis on points in the supervisor's or company's favor. But overstatement or overcommitment or strict one-sidedness is likely to be rejected immediately or to lead to disillusionment later when events do not confirm the supervisor's word.

To recapitulate, training in interviewing starts with (1) a lesson in semantic difficulties and an emphasis on the use of questions for clarification, and (2) guided practice in role-playing general-purpose interviews. Once the new supervisor has acquired insight and moderate skill in interviewing techniques (for transmitting information, eliciting information, and making a case), he is ready for further development of these skills in substantive subjects—through case discussions and role playing in courses on labor relations, safety, training, and so forth. In this way, the vehicular function of the interview course is accomplished. These skills will come into play in almost every activity the supervisor performs:

1. The technique of transmitting information is useful in virtually all supervisory functions involving employees, especially in giving directions, orders, assignments, instructions, safety pointers, and induction information.
2. The technique of eliciting information is crucial to handling grievances, disciplinary cases, and unsafe acts.
3. The technique of making a convincing case comes into play in matters of rates, workloads, work assignments, and personnel and other actions.

In the substantive courses, these basic techniques will help the new supervisor master the full-blown interviewing skills needed for various job situations. The beginning skills acquired in the interviewing course should be highly transferable to these later training applications and to the job itself. Certain situations may call for a single approach primarily; others may require a combination of telling, receiving, and convincing. It is to the application in specific job-related situations that role playing and on-the-job coaching should be directed. What techniques or intermixture will serve in a particular situation? This is the question to which substantive training and coaching will address themselves. But there must be something in the supervisor's repertoire to apply. Hence the value of an underlying course in interviewing.

INFORMATION AT A TIME OF CHANGE

Nowhere is the careful use of information more important than in the explanation of change. The new supervisor must realize that an ambiguous situation invites a subjective evaluation by the employee that is based on the employee's own needs and attitudes. He will size up the change in terms of the relative advantage or disadvantage to him, as he perceives it, and act accordingly—on a scale from enthusiastic acceptance and support to outright rejection and active opposition. If the employee sees matters wrongly, he is likely to act wrongly. He may postpone judgment in order to secure information, and this very search for clarification may give the appearance of opposition. The supervisor's task is to inform the employee of the change and its expected effect in such a way that the employee can make a realistic appraisal of the situation as his basis for action.

The interview should take into account the employee's view of the probable impact of the change on himself. Different views will require different treatment by the supervisor.

Problems can arise when the employee expects a larger benefit from the change than will be available or expects (erroneously) to be harmed by it. In the first case, the supervisor should pare down the employee's expectations to realistic proportions; the truth may be less pleasing to the employee, but misleading him is ultimately more damaging. In the second case, the supervisor should cite the advantages of the change to the employee without overselling him.

If the employee is apprehensive because of harmful effects from similar changes in the past, the supervisor should help the employee distinguish between his past experience and his present situation. The objective is to help the employee evaluate the change in terms of current circumstances and predictable consequences. Of course, the good results expected to flow from the change must be confirmed by the employee's new experience.

The interview is especially difficult when the change is going to be unfavorable to the employee, and both he and the supervisor correctly perceive it as such. The recommended course is to be realistic, even though it is painful to both parties, and to give the employee a positive choice if one exists. Often certain options are available, not all of which are strongly unfavorable. If a relatively good option exists that reduces the harmful effect, the supervisor should help the employee to see it—but not to see more than is there.

Job Organization

The new supervisor must organize the many activities necessary for carrying out his functions and meeting his responsibilities. He must devise a routine so that the job can be performed day in and day out. Thus training must prepare the new supervisor to schedule tasks and allocate his time so as to bring efficiency into his total operation.

A simple course in so-called time management is no answer, although pointers from such a course would be helpful. A more comprehensive and job-specific approach is required: a lining up of supervisory activities to determine which must be scheduled at exact intervals and which occur unpredictably but nevertheless require some allocation of time. Length of time as well as frequency can be set for certain activities. Allowance must be made for demands placed on the supervisor by other people; meetings called by the department head are a prime example. Staff contacts should also be taken into account. If clerical help is provided, decisions need to be made on assignment of tasks and delegation of duties.

To begin bringing the job into administrative compass, the new

supervisor needs classroom instruction from an experienced supervisor. Such training will prepare the trainee for organizing his job as he moves into the full assignment under the guidance of a coach. Without this preparation as a framework, experiences under early coaching may appear disjointed and the coaching itself may be less meaningful.

It is generally assumed that the supervisory job can be managed. But this is not automatically so. The new supervisor, left to his own resources, may find it impossible to bring the job under control. Even with help, the process of job organization is a developmental one; it is perhaps ultimately the key issue, since job mastery is impossible without job organizaton. Training in job organization should therefore be a long-term effort. It should extend beyond coaching to periodic diagnostic appraisals of the new supervisor's performance in order to identify and gird up those aspects of performance which make full control difficult and to produce balanced execution which encompasses all job tasks and gives appropriate weight to each.

CHAPTER 4

The Pervasive Subject: Motivation

WHAT should we teach a new supervisor about motivation? So much has been written about motivation—much of it established now as inviolable doctrine—that it is difficult to dig through the staggering mass of material to uncover items of practical value to the supervisor. Unfortunately, much of the writing has been based on clinical experience with disturbed people or children rather than on industrial experience with "normal" employees; some of it represents theoretical models that have not been tested by research; and some of it is armchair speculation arising from unstructured observations. Research studies themselves, though many of them are admirable, may suffer from weaknesses in experimental design or from unwarranted generalization of findings.

The Search for a Workable Model

The trainer who is unwilling or unable to delve with a critical eye, who is not himself a trained psychologist and must rely on the current motivational literature to guide him, is faced with a set of "givens." These, in effect, are articles of faith underlying recommended courses of action in motivating employees. Not many industrial practitioners have the temerity—or background—to question their validity. So, as gospel, the trainer must first believe:

1. That Theory Y is superior to Theory X. (The gospel according to McGregor.)
2. That there is a hierarchy of needs. (The gospel according to Maslow.)
3. That motivators are distinct from hygiene factors. (The gospel according to Herzberg.)
4. That a 9–9 on the managerial grid represents the best way of managing. (The gospel according to Blake.)

The litany of "I believes" goes on and on. The problem is not that the gospels lack truth (there is some truth apparently in each of them). Rather, the problem lies in accepting such a gospel package as a total working model for motivating employees. If a trainer is not equipped to evaluate the sources of the doctrines, he can at least test them against the lessons of his own experience and good sense.

One lesson he will have learned is humility. He knows that motivation is complex, that people are complex, and that a major element in that complexity is individual differences. The same formula will not work for everyone. He knows, too, that his influence is limited. He does not teach motives to employees. He can, however, provide certain incentives that might elicit satisfactory performance—with the realization that he may not have the rewards available which all employees will consider worth the effort.

The supervisor needs a valid and useful view of motivation, one that represents a substantially true reading of employees and that is within his control—that is, within his capacity as a supervisor to utilize. These are the criteria a practical model of motivation must meet. He should not be saddled with a variety of motivational theories, some of which conflict, most of which fail to meet the tests of validity and control, and none of which he or his trainer can fully understand. So, without denying the merits of other approaches or the existence of more deeply imbedded bases for employee behavior, the supervisor will find it useful to focus on the cognitive aspects of motivation, relying on the assumption that employees will make choices which they believe are to their advantage; that they will expect certain results from what they do; and that they will have preferences among such results and will act accordingly. It is a matter, in short, of making conscious choices.

This is not an all-encompassing approach, tidily packaged. Some things will hang out. If there are other bases for an employee's behavior, the supervisor may be at a loss. But he cannot absolutely understand or control employee behavior in any event, and we have done well enough as trainers if we provide him with a valid means of influencing a significant part of employee behavior. Such influence can be exerted if the supervisor deals with employees' conscious choices through his effect on the rewarding outcomes and on the perceptions and expectations of employees regarding such outcomes.

This approach is not intended to deny the influence of the employee's past. But it does attempt to focus the employee's attention on a correct sizing-up of advantages here and now and to correct any misinterpretations (through information and later confirmation) if the employee bases his evaluation on past experience. The supervisor simply cannot deal with the employee's past in any other terms.

A useful framework, therefore, for exercising supervisory influence is one that relates performance (and behavior in general) to individual expectations and satisfactions. The employee comes to the job with his own motivational mix, or general set of needs. If he is to be motivated, he must expect to work out satisfactorily on the job and expect, too, that if he does work out there will be some rewards in it for him that satisfy his strong needs. If the motivation to perform indeed depends on these factors (which appears to be so, in considerable part), the supervisor is in a fortunate position, since he has some influence on both the employee's expectations and his rewards. Here, in simple form, is the motivational framework the supervisor might profitably use:

Expectation of   Expectation
mastering the job   of rewards
Employee ————————————→ Mastery of job ————————————→ Rewards

This chapter will examine the specific actions a supervisor might take at various points in the motivational process.*

Expectation of Mastering the Job

Obviously, the effort an employee is likely to exert will depend, early in the game, on whether he expects to make a go of it. He may appraise the job erroneously, seeing its requirements as insurmountable on the one hand or undemanding on the other. Employees differ, of course, in their goals, levels of aspiration, and willingness to take risks. The supervisor's task is to give the employee comprehensive and realistic information on what is required on the job. This process should begin before hiring and should proceed well into early training so that the applicant can adequately determine whether the position is for him. If he regards the job with extensive misgivings or with indifference—seeing its requirements accurately—the job is probably unsuitable and he should not go into it. But if he bases his judgment on inaccurate or incomplete information and accepts the job, the supervisor will be hard put to counter his false expectations. When the realities of the job are not in keeping with his expectations, his motivation and effort will inevitably suffer. It is precisely when information is minimal that the employee is likely to color his evaluation with his own wants and attitudes.

* See John P. Campbell, Marvin D. Dunnette, Edward E. Lawler III, and Karl E. Weick, Jr., *Managerial Behavior, Performance, and Effectiveness* (New York: McGraw-Hill Book Company, 1970), pp. 345–348, for a discussion of a "hybrid expectancy" model of motivation. This model is a major source—supplemented and modified on the basis of experience—of motivational views taken in this chapter.

The supervisor can influence the employee's expectations about the job early in the hiring stage by:

1. Matching the employee to the job, in terms of abilities and interests, as best he can.
2. Defining the job and the role of the employee.
3. Indicating what help the supervisor will give him to become adept in the job.
4. Exposing him to a model—an employee who has acquired competency.

Of course, as the employee moves into the job and develops skill, the supervisor will have to redefine his expanding role. But it is unwise to allow the employee to set his foot inside the door until he has a clear and realistic idea of what to expect when he does come in.

Helping the Employee Master the Job

Once the employee is on the job, the supervisor can exert a strong influence on his achievement through such actions as these:

1. Giving him adequate training and attention.
2. Giving him pertinent information, especially feedback on progress.
3. Helping him adjust to job requirements and conditions. The supervisor should make the job as manageable as possible and conditions as predictable and controllable as he can.
4. Helping him establish relationships with fellow employees.
5. Helping him with personal problems (within limits) that have a bearing on job performance—primarily, listening to him and referring him to professional sources of help.

The subjects of training and feedback are discussed elsewhere, but the motivational aspects of learning need to be emphasized at this point. The experience of success is intrinsically rewarding, and the supervisor should do everything he can to bring it about. He should also recognize success. Feedback, particularly the positive kind we refer to as reinforcement, is motivating. Later in training, when job skills are under control, reinforcement should still be given, but intermittently, to help ensure the employee's persistence; it can have such an effect.

One of the major values of successful performance is that it breeds expectations of further success—of further mastery of job assignments. These expectations derive, of course, from the employee's previous experience, and as indicated above they can be influenced to some extent before training begins. But the accomplishment of the trainee is the primary influence. Thus the supervisor should help him achieve repeated successes to enhance this expectation. The results, which will be instrumental to his development, include (1) a self-assurance on the part of the employee that continued effort will bring success in new activities, and (2) an overriding of the negative effects of occasional failure. Timing is important here; if significant setbacks occur before the expectations of mastery become strong, the learning of subsequent tasks can be impaired.*

An often overlooked influence on motivation is the job itself—not the basic fit of the job to the employee (important in itself as a source of intrinsic satisfaction) but the very shape and structure of the job, its manageability. Sometimes jobs are built out of an ill-assorted set of tasks and responsibilities, the tag ends or overflow of other jobs that people have despaired of performing or a combination of new and ill-defined tasks that has been forced on the department. Sometimes, too many uncontrollable and unpredictable contingencies are left in the job, or the employee is placed in an organizational limbo where reporting and feedback relationships are complex or fuzzy. Or the employee is simply ignored. Although a few employees seem to thrive in uncertainty, most need to be assigned to clear and manageable duties, however broad, and to be

* See Albert Bandura, *Social Learning* (Englewood Cliffs, N.J.: Prentice-Hall, 1977), pp. 79–85, for a discussion of efficacy expectations. The author's experience gives support to Bandura's views on this subject and the general subject of modeling. They are highly pertinent in the training of new supervisors.

anchored by solid lines to a relatively fixed organizational chart and communications network. An unmanageable job defies learning and thwarts the experience of success that is so critical to the employee's expectations of further accomplishment.

If an employee, despite his best effort, feels that he still cannot run the job or if he continues to flounder among relationships that do not provide the required guidance and feedback, he is likely to leave. Few employees will willingly persist in a losing battle. Pleasant associations with other employees may make the struggle a little more tolerable, but this satisfaction is unlikely to hold the employee for very long in a job which neither he nor anyone else can run. The job is the thing, and frustrations arising from its unmanageability are likely to be the major influence. Most likely, the employee will leave the job quickly on his own. Or he may persist in it with a developing aggression that so exacerbates his working relationships that he will eventually have to be removed.

Expectation of Rewards

Although so-called contingency contracts with employees (you do so-and-so and you will receive such-and-such in return) can become childish if carried too far, the supervisor should indicate to the employee the sort of performance he wants, specify what rewards will then be forthcoming, and use those rewards to shape performance. In this process the supervisor goes beyond an explanation of the employee's role and the help he can expect in carrying it out to a clear statement of what is "in it" for him if he does carry it out. In short, the supervisor influences not only the employee's expectations of achievement but his expectations of related rewards as well.

The organization provides certain rewards that are tied to minimal performance requirements—such rewards as the company benefits of hospitalization, life insurance, pensions, and vacation. These rewards are usually contingent on satisfactory completion of an eligibility period and demand no more than minimally acceptable job performance permitting continued employment. Job security in terms of job rights acquired after a probationary period is a similar type of reward, useful primarily in eliciting adequate performance in the early period of employment. Rewards of this sort are outside the supervisor's jurisdiction to give, although he is involved in administering them (making sure that the minimum requirements are met) and can use them as early reinforcers.

Other rewards, such as pay and promotion, are more contingent on levels of performance and are within the supervisor's control to some degree. Such reinforcers as approval, praise, recognition, and favorable comment can be applied to any aspect or level of performance and are completely within the supervisor's power and freedom to use.

Before the employee is hired, he should be informed of the tangible extrinsic rewards (pay, benefits, promotional opportunities) attached to performance, with an emphasis on that very attachment. The rewards should not be treated as isolated satisfactions. The employee should be given a clear idea of expected performance, expected rewards, and the connection between them. And, early in his association with the employee, the supervisor should begin to indicate what sort of performance will bring his approval. We pay dearly if a new employee misperceives the rewards available to him and the bases for them in performance. Our early hiring efforts may lead to such misjudgments if, for example, we use the reward "package" as a lure without mentioning the requirement of performance, or if, in our frantic efforts to fill openings, we neglect the applicant's need for a clear appraisal of the job. Of course, misperceptions may arise later in the game. The giving of information on performance expectations is a continuing activity; the information should be updated as the employee moves forward in his job.

The giving of information, early and progressively, on job performance is among the substantive activities involved in inducting employees, and we have examined the subject in that context. But in the context of motivation, the matter of primary importance is the linking of performance and rewards, and the chief function of the information provided by the supervisor is to clarify this contingency. The employee should have no doubt about what he is being rewarded for.

Confusion can arise. Praising and recognizing an employee for certain aspects of job performance and recommending a pay increase or promotion on other bases can lead to erroneous perceptions, with a resultantly lopsided job effort aimed at attaining the more powerful reinforcers, as the employee gauges them. Moreover, praise and recognition divorced from tangible rewards may become empty verbal exercises with small motivational effect on an employee who values tangible rewards. If a model is used as a representation of rewarded performance, the employee serving as model should actually perform the job at a high level and should be seen as deriving satisfaction from it. If the new employee gets the impression, through association with a model or other employees, that rewards are not dependent on performance, that they are not given when performance is good or are given on other bases (favoritism, nepotism) or capriciously, he is not likely to be motivated toward excellent job performance. The supervisor himself is often at fault for rewarding employees without regard to performance, thus undermining the potentially favorable effect of rewards based on performance. An employee is influenced not only by what he is told but by what he observes and particularly by what he experiences. Consistency among these indications is needed to firm up the contingency between rewards and performance.

It is obvious that the employee's perception plays a crucial role in his behavior, particularly his perception of rewards available to him. This perception is at the heart of the interaction between the individual and the job; the employee's behavior flows largely from how he sizes up the situation. And it is for the purpose of providing a sounder basis for perception of the current situation that the supervisor should use valid information. The supervisor's task is to bring realism to bear on the employee's perception and to counter possible misperceptions stemming from the employee's past experience and training and his wants and attitudes, all of which affect perception. The transmittal of information on job performance requirements and related rewards can be discussed and practiced in interview training. But the role of perception in human behavior, which the supervisor must understand, should be discussed in the context of motivation.

Providing the Rewards

If the employee's expectations of rewards are not met in the job, his efforts are likely to flag—if he remains in the job at all. The supervisor's task at this stage is to see that the rewards are given. He is not the only source of tangible rewards, but he does have influence—a direct influence on pay level and job assignments and a contributing voice in promotion when openings occur in his department.

Since pay and promotion are delayed rewards, they may not serve as efficiently as reinforcers of performance as the more immediate intangible rewards of supervisory approval and recognition. The latter are more readily at the supervisor's disposal. He should use his influence judiciously, offering such reinforcers to bring about the sort of behavior and performance he wants. The rewards should be geared to an increasingly higher level of performance—but withholding deserved rewards altogether can destroy motivation.

Although some confidence in the efficacy of reinforcers is justified, blind and mechanistic use of them as a sure-fire cure for performance problems is definitely unwarranted. There are still many unanswered questions concerning the nature and effect of reinforcers. We can perhaps more readily demonstrate their usefulness in teaching the job than in sustaining job performance.

The sustaining of motivation and performance is a complex matter. On the one hand, we are told that rewarded behavior tends to recur and, on the other hand, that satisfaction can have a negative effect on motivation. The supervisor needs to ask: Which motives? Which rewards? Which individual? In some cases, a satisfaction or reward will increase motivation, because the employee then aspires to a higher goal. But goal setting differs among individuals, and some motives are satisfied by the maintenance of the status quo rather than by the attainment of ever higher goals. In addition, people attach different motives to the same rewards or different rewards to the same motive. We will examine some of these issues later in the light of research indications.

The strength of a reward is a highly personal matter. The reward may be seen as satisfying in itself. It may be traded off with other rewards (or nonrewards) as a determinant of performance. It may serve as a means of attaining larger goals related to the employee's personal life, his family, or his place in the community. If it does serve as such, it is likely to exert a heavier and longer pull on performance.

The strength of a reward is largely beyond the supervisor's influence. He cannot dictate the importance of the reward to the employee—what it should mean to him in itself or as an instrument for higher satisfaction. The supervisor's constructive actions have run their course when he has:

1. Indicated to the employee what the rewards are and what sort of performance they are contingent upon.
2. Assisted the employee, through training, to reach a competent level of performance so that he is in position to reach for the rewards in their fullest.
3. Assured, within the limits of his power, that the rewards are forthcoming.

The supervisor should be realistic in anticipating results from this approach, taking account of individual differences. He cannot expect to provide sustaining satisfactions for all employees. After he has expended his best efforts, skillful as they are, an employee may still leave. Often the employee simply concludes at the end, having had his eyes open all the way, that there is just not enough in it for him after all. The supervisor who has genuine insights into employee motivation will not despair at this point but will remain convinced that his effect on an employee's motivation, though not always compelling and perhaps less so later in the game, is still significant.

The expanded motivational model in Figure 1 shows the progressive stages of the employee's development and actions that the supervisor can take at each step in regard to employee expectations and rewards.*

* The figure was developed from a hybrid expectancy model of work motivation in Campbell, *op. cit.*, p. 347. (The development involved modification and expansion for the purpose of listing task goals and rewards and of indicating supervisory actions that affect expectancies, goal attainment, and rewards.)

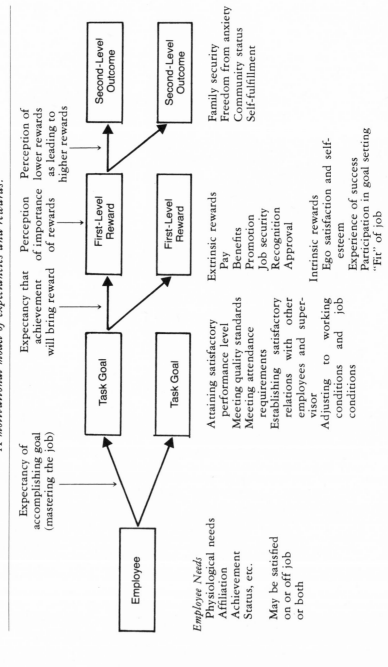

FIGURE 1.

A motivational model of expectancies and rewards.

FIGURE 1, *cont.*

Supervisory Actions Influence employee's expectancy of achievement:	Clear way for learning and running job:	Influence expectancy of rewards:	Provide rewards:	In general: Maximize rewards Influence expectancies
1. Match trainee to job (abilities and interest) as much as possible	1. Adequate training and attention	1. Indicate what the extrinsic rewards are and what they are contingent upon (as basis for decision on accepting job)	1. See that extrinsic rewards are forthcoming (including reinforcement from supervisor)	
2. Define job and role of employee	2. Information, including adequate feedback on progress	2. Expose employee to model (another employee who gets satisfaction from job)	2. Influence intrinsic rewards as much as possible	
3. Indicate help to be given	3. Help with adjustment to job and job conditions; make job manageable and conditions predictable or controllable			
4. Expose him to a model (employee who has "made it")	4. Help with adjustment to other employees			
	5. Help with personal problems (within limits) bearing on performance			

CHAPTER 5

Arranging
the Training Program

ONCE we have determined what the new supervisor needs, our task is to devise a training plan to cover those needs. In the process, some degree of translation will be required. The terms we have used to identify needs do not necessarily become the titles of courses, but we must ensure that all the identified needs are covered in our training program.

Covering the Ground

A major consideration is that we move progressively from (1) the initial stage of giving background information and, when needed, background skills, to (2) the early stage of application through the outlining of procedures, to (3) the intermediate stage of application through discussion and role playing, to (4) the advanced stage of application through experience on the job itself under coaching. With certain subjects, one or more earlier steps may be omitted, but coaching is a requirement in all aspects of the job. And, generally speaking, we proceed from giving knowledge to discussing and acting out the handling of situations to providing guided performance on the job.

Classroom lectures, with illustrations, will serve for imparting background knowledge and outlining procedures. The classroom "action" phase includes role playing and discussion, using realistic case material. Discussion will be useful in teaching procedures not requiring a significant amount of interpersonal contact. Role playing is recommended when interchanges with employees are an essential part of the skill to be developed. Of course, role playing will involve discussion as well, especially in determining applicable procedures and in summing up. The dual approach, using both techniques, is a "natural" for any interpersonal procedure; the class can be charged with deciding what to do and then with doing it. On the job itself, coaching is the irreplaceable technique.

Until the coaching stage is reached, classroom sessions will serve the learning objective, with the major exception of the development of background skill in operating and maintaining machinery. This technical skill can be attained only by training on the machinery itself and by performing key jobs. (Preparatory or supplementary class sessions are useful for teaching terminology and principles and for specifying procedures required in setting up the machines and diagnosing malfunctions.) Other background skills will require visits to production departments for completion of class-initiated assignments. These include conducting laboratory tests, establishing job methods, making time studies and job evaluations, drawing up a training plan, instructing employees, making safety inspections, and inspecting materials in process.

Cases for role playing and discussion in the action phase of classroom training can be readily developed within the company. In labor relations, for example, there is a rich store of case material in the records of grievances and disciplinary actions. In some subjects (safety, for example) pertinent case material is available from commercial sources.

When cases are used, small-group discussion and multiple role playing are recommended to give all class members an opportunity to participate and practice. In role playing, a playback of the interview on TV tape is an excellent device, along with a critique from the direct observer, for giving the trainee insight into the effectiveness of his performance and for diagnosing what went wrong.

If there are not enough new supervisors or trainees to make up a class (as sometimes occurs in small companies), the classroom aspect of the program can be handled in part by consultations with operating and staff personnel. Under such circumstances, a heavier burden will fall on coaching—and on the printed word, which is still a good means of instruction if review and clarification through consultation are also provided.

Selection of Instructors and Coaches

For substantive courses, instructors should be recruited from within the organization. Staff personnel responsible for certain programs and systems can be called in to outline policies and procedures which involve the particular functional area—labor relations, quality control, safety, and so forth. With applications and cases, however, it is advisable to have a line manager (head of a department or plant) handle the sessions, since he will command credibility as a solver of practical problems.

For the vehicular subjects of problem solving, decision making, and interviewing, people within the organization can be used, if they are competent in these processes. Otherwise, outside help— which is in plentiful supply—should be sought. We tend to underestimate the competence of in-company people in such subjects and endow outsiders readily and uncritically with expertise. Advance examination of the outsider's credentials is in order, not only to ensure an effective presentation but also to make sure that he covers the field we want and is not peddling a pet technique or some current evanescent fad. For instruction in job organization, line managers with recognized success at managing the supervisory job should be used.

The selection of an instructor for the subject of motivation depends on our training objective. If we are concerned with a review of motivational theory or with instruction in a model representing the new fashion (transactional analysis, for example), an outside academician or consultant will serve. But, as stated earlier, we must provide the new supervisor with a valid and practical view of employee motivation—one that also fits in reasonably well with the organization's values and policies. A model that is based on expectations and rewards and that stresses the cognitive aspects of motivation will make sense to most organizations.

Thus the most highly recommended instructor in motivation is an inside person who knows the organizational climate thoroughly and who can present a model that the supervisor will find within his control and likely to work for him. (We examined such a model in Chapter 4.) The instructor should also have a sound background in psychology, with a broad and critical perspective that will prevent him from trying to apply the model too rigidly.

In-company people should be trained for classroom instructing, but we should not expect to transform our functional experts into highly proficient teachers, especially when a considerable number of them are used in the program. Skills of presentation and discussion can be sharpened, but we should be sure to allocate enough of the available time to instructional outlines, materials, and visuals. If we can thus help the temporary instructor organize his message, an acceptable course is likely to ensue. Feedback from early efforts will aid improvement.

Coaches, of course, should be inside people, either experienced first-line supervisors or heads of the departments in which the new supervisors are assigned. Unfortunately, a good supervisor is not necessarily a good coach; it is therefore important to train people carefully for the coaching role. Training will be much more extensive than that provided to classroom instructors, since coaching requires a wide range of knowledge, skills, and techniques (explanation, modeling, cueing, appraising, feedback, and reinforcement). The coach should be adept at interviewing and problem solving and expert in the technical aspects of manufacturing. Some potential coaches will already possess these skills through experience, but in most cases much remains to be learned. The gaps should be identified and filled in before the coaching assignment.

The experienced older supervisor especially may need help; his self-taught coaching efforts are often shallow gestures, leaving the trainee to pick things up largely on his own.

A common misconception about coaching is that it is intended to evoke exact imitation, that the trainee should mimic the gestures, modes of expression, and other mannerisms of the coach. Modeling, of course, does not occur without a personal style. We cannot ask the coach to perform in an atypical way when he has a trainee in tow. But he must help the new supervisor discriminate between those actions that represent a workable basic model—which the new supervisor can copy in his own manner—and those special encrustations of the coach that are not to be imitated. This is a difficult distinction to make, since style is a subtle combination of all performance characteristics. Yet the distinction can be drawn. For example, in handling a complaint or grievance, the coach will carry out a certain course of action: investigating the factual source of the grievance, arriving at a decision, and rendering and recording the decision. The coach will try to demonstrate for the trainee effective execution of procedures and effective communication with the employee. Admittedly, the coach will start from an established relationship with the employee which the new supervisor does not have, and this relationship will influence his handling of the problem. But there is still a substantial series of actions available for fruitful imitation, no matter what the difference in background and personality between coach and trainee. And in the explanation of each step, the coach can identify and emphasize those imitable portions that are effective.

There are rules, principles, and concepts which the modeling should make clear. Thus we get behind the head wagging, joking, desk tapping, coin jiggling, and other mannerisms of the coach to the solid stuff of skillful activity which we are trying to prime the new supervisor to use.

The possibility that the trainee will pick up mannerisms is increased if the coach makes the mistake of overplaying the demonstration. The trainee is not learning a dramatic part line by line and gesture by gesture. Modeling should give the trainee a conceptual grasp of how to proceed, and then practice should begin. It is at this stage, when the trainee starts handling matters and the modeled performance is put to use, that the skill emerges. And it is at this point that the full battery of other coaching techniques is wheeled into play—the cueing, feedback, and reinforcement, specifically—to expedite the development of skill.

Outline of Topic Coverage by Classroom Techniques

Now that we have examined the topics for coverage in training the new supervisor and explored what can be accomplished in the classroom and on the job, we are ready to combine the two in outline form. Table 6 shows which aspect of each subject (substantive, vehicular, and pervasive) can be taught in the classroom by lecture, discussion, role playing, and practice and, as an extension, by out-of-class assignments. The outline represents a "working paper" for aligning training needs (now couched, perhaps, in different terms) with specific classroom teaching techniques. On the basis of such data, the training courses can be constructed. Later in the chapter we will examine the topics and activities to be covered in on-the-job coaching.

Training Program Schedule

The final step in setting up a training program is to devise a schedule—one that moves in an orderly way from technology to systems and procedures, to vehicular and pervasive subjects (problem solving, decision making, interviewing, motivation), to application of procedures through discussion and role playing of cases, to job organization principles, and finally to coaching on the job. Obviously the phases exist in a hierarchy: technology and systems are the structuring basis of the supervisor's job; familiarity with systems and procedures should precede application, as should the vehicular subjects (except job organization) and motivation; a grasp of the principles of job organization should precede guidance in

(Text continues page 117.)

TABLE 6.

Outline of training subjects and coverage by classroom techniques.

Training Subject	Lecture	Discussion	Role Playing	Practice in Class	Outside Assignment
Operation and maintenance of machinery	Terminology Principles of operation Procedures for making settings and diagnosing malfunctions Standards of efficiency and output				Operating and repairing machinery (extensive period in production department)
Cost control	Cost system Content of cost reports and related operational reports	Cases involving cost-effective decisions in various operational situations		Work up cost figures for a department	
Quality control	Quality standards and product specifications Control system (testing, inspection, feedback, and recording procedures)				Operation of laboratory equipment Performance of in-process inspections

Safety and health	Accident causation Safety procedures (preventive, investigative, reporting) Costs and liability; compensation provisions Health protection procedures (provisions of industrial hygiene program: respiration, hearing, and other matters) Characteristics of materials (effects on employees) OSHA provisions and standards Security organization, systems, and procedures	Cases of accidents for determining causes and corrective measures Cases of security incidents.	Correction of unsafe acts Instruction of employees in hazards and unsafe acts	Filling out accident report forms	Conducting inspections
Utilizing and compensating employees	Job methods procedures Job evaluation procedures Rate-setting procedures (including time study) Provisions governing rates for reporting time, overtime,	Cases for determining pay rates applicable to special situations	Preparing employee for time study Explaining time study results Explaining changes in rate or workload	Making methods study, evaluating job, and making time study (simple or contrived task)	Making methods study, evaluating job, and making time study (actual job in production department)

TABLE 6, cont.

Training Subject	Lecture	Discussion	Role Playing	Practice in Class	Outside Assignment
	waiting time, temp. transfers, nonstandard conditions, shift premiums, and related matters				
	Union contract and company policy on rates and workloads				
	Contract and policy on job and shift rights				
	Timekeeping and payroll system				
	Company or plant rules governing paycheck distribution				
Labor relations	Personnel policies and procedures (including discipline)	Cases on pertinent rules, clause, or requirement applying to situation and on action to take	Hearing complaints and grievances		
	Union contract provisions	Cases on hiring, transfer, and promotion decisions	Handling disciplinary cases		
	EEO requirements				
	Contents of turnover and absentee reports				

Subject					
Job skills training	Principles of learning and instruction (including reinforcement) Content of training programs Learning difficulties and diagnostic methods to identify causes	Cases on principles pertinent to learning situations or problems and how to apply them	Handling cases of performance problems involving learning difficulties	Instructing in simple tasks	Instructing in job tasks Drawing up training plan for an actual job
Induction training	Induction procedures and rationale Contents of information checklists Procedures for reviewing progress		Giving induction information Discussing progress in training period		
Problem solving and decision making	Models for problem solving ("physical" and performance problems) Models for decision making	Cases for determining causes of problems and deciding on remedial action	Cases of performance problems (involving interaction with employee)		
Interviewing	Difficulties of communication and causes Interviewing procedures	Cases involving breakdown in communications	Cases involving giving information, eliciting information, and influencing attitudes		
Motivation	Motivational principles and model Related principles of perception and reinforcement	Cases involving behavior or performance for analysis of motivational problems			
Job organization	Job duties and activities, scheduling of activities, setting of priorities, and use of time				

FIGURE 2.

Training program schedule (showing progressive phases and subjects covered in each).

PHASE 1: MANUFACTURING TECHNOLOGY
  Subject   Operation and maintenance of equipment

PHASE 2: SYSTEMS, POLICIES, PROCEDURES, AND CONTROLS (substantive subjects, factual coverage)
  Subjects
    Quality control
    Cost control
    Safety and health
    Security
    Industrial engineering (utilizing employees)
    Labor relations
      Material: *Handling Grievances: A Guide for Management and Labor,* Trotta (BNA)
    Skills training
      Material: *Helping Employees Develop Job Skill,* Gardner (BNA)
    Induction training

PHASE 3: VEHICULAR SUBJECTS AND MOTIVATION
  Subjects
    Interviewing
      Material: *Handling Barriers in Communication,* Lee and Lee (Harper)
      Film: *Avoiding Communication Breakdown* (BNA)
    Problem solving and decision making
      Material: *The Rational Manager,* Kepner and Tregoe (McGraw-Hill)
      Solving Managerial Problems, Laird and Grote (Addison-Wesley)
    Performance problems
      Material: *Analyzing Performance Problems,* Mager and Pipe (Fearon)
      An Ounce of Analysis, Harless (Harless Performance Guild)
    Motivation
      Material: *Managerial Behavior, Performance, and Effectiveness,* Campbell, Dunnette, Lawler, and Weick (McGraw-Hill)
      Films: *Man on the Assembly Line* (McGraw-Hill)
      The Way I See It (Roundtable)
      Overcoming Resistance to Change (Roundtable)
      Who Did What to Whom? (Research Press)
      The Rewards of Rewarding (Roundtable)

PHASE 4: APPLICATIONS OF PROCEDURES AND CONTROLS (cases for discussion or role playing)

Subjects

Grievance cases, disciplinary cases, and other labor relations cases
Material: *Supervisor's Handbook on Insubordination,*
Trotta (BNA)
Film: *A Case of Insubordination* (Roundtable)
Cases on efficiency and quality problems
Cases on employee performance
Cases involving unsafe acts
Material: *Safety Training for the Supervisor,* Gardner (Addison-Wesley)
Cases involving security incidents
Cost cases
Cases involving job standards (rates and workloads) and changes in standards
Mixed cases (involving a wide range of supervisory activities)
Material—in-basket cases:
General Machine Corporation (University of Michigan, Bureau of Industrial Relations)
Missile Propulsion Division (University of Michigan, Bureau of Industrial Relations)

PHASE 5: JOB ORGANIZATION

PHASE 6: COACHING ON THE JOB

---

running the job; and the final training phase, to which all others are preliminary, is coaching on the job itself.

Figure 2 outlines such a schedule and lists commercial materials (books and films) that I have found useful in teaching certain subjects, as a supplement to company-developed materials.

The time devoted to each phase will depend on the importance and complexity of the topics and on how much practice is needed in application. The technical training requirements will depend not only on the complexity of the manufacturing operations but also on the experience of the new supervisor. Obviously, a trainee promoted from within the department will need less technical training than someone hired from outside or transferred from another department. The claim of experience in a supposedly related operation elsewhere should always be examined critically; an assumption that skill is transferable is often unfounded.

Classroom coverage (Phases 2 through 5) can usually be accomplished in two to three weeks of full-time training. The coaching phase should last for several months, long enough for the new supervisor to master routine tasks and to handle a substantial number of problems. Within this period, the coach will gradually withdraw his attention (reentering the scene when new situations arise); and, if he has done his job well, he will need to provide only intermittent reinforcement to keep alive the activities of the new supervisor which have already become effective. As a supplement to coaching, periodic consultations with staff experts should be arranged for the new supervisor for clarification of persisting questions of administration or technology.

Within Phases 2, 3, or 4 of classroom training, it is not necessary to complete one topic before going to another. Subjects can be scheduled for different times of the same day—a procedure that will relieve fatigue and space out learning. Job organization can be attached to Phase 4 as a late course in the series of cases; however, it should not precede coaching by too long a period. In the case-handling phase, specific kinds of cases (grievances, safety, performance problems, quality) should be worked through before moving to mixed cases of the type encountered by a supervisor in a typical day on the job.

The supervisor should be given classroom training before he is put on the job or—if a slot must be filled before formal training is available—as soon thereafter as possible. If there is too long a delay between job assignment and formal training, the new supervisor will get locked into a job he is seen as "running"—though in most cases he is actually managing by trial and error—and it is difficult to pry him loose for the comprehensive training he needs to operate effectively. In large companies, the classroom phases can be repeated two or three times a year in a central location, so that no new supervisor is on the job very long before training becomes available. When openings can be anticipated, as in the case of retirements, there is no excuse for placing a new supervisor on the job without training.

Some trainers may argue that classroom training should be broken up to give new supervisors a "short taste" of the job after they have completed the courses in systems and procedures and before they tackle application, with the expectation that the cases will become more meaningful. There is some merit in this view. Unfortunately, it is difficult to organize the short tasting experience so that it benefits learning, and often the short stay stretches out indefinitely. Even at the expense of losing the advantages of spaced learning, we do better to hold the trainee for the full treatment if we can.

Most of the materials used in the substantive courses should be developed in the company itself (some will already be available). It is the company's procedures we are teaching, and a statement of these procedures becomes our textbook. Cases involving procedural and interpersonal activities should also be prepared inside. However, there is good material available, in print and on film, from commercial sources for teaching the nonsubstantive subjects of interviewing, problem solving, decision making, and motivation. And a few books and films are pertinent enough for the substantive courses—specifically, employee training, safety, and labor relations. Marketed material that I have found especially relevant and helpful is listed in the schedule given earlier.

Coaching on the Job

Since coaching on the job is the climactic training experience, essential to the full development of the supervisory skills and to mastery of the total job, an expanded discussion is in order. A suggested schedule and outline of a coaching arrangement for a new supervisor in a production department is given below. A major feature of the schedule is the stage-by-stage movement into the full job. The supervisory job is too complex to be thrown at the trainee all at once, even under the best of coaches and with the best of classroom and technical preparation.

GENERAL SHAPE AND PRINCIPLES OF A COACHING APPROACH

Coaching is the rather broad technique of developing the subordinate's skills and improving his performance through modeling and guided experience on the job. Here are some elements of the process, as applied to a "green" subordinate:

1. The learning process must be gradual—step by step. Routine assignments or job tasks should be covered first. More help should be given in the early stages, with real assurance of success provided at each stage.

2. Successful performance should be reinforced. The coach needs to have reliable information on the trainee's performance. He must give immediate feedback, making his best judgment on the effectiveness or ineffectiveness of the trainee's actions even though ultimate results are not even discernible. Those actions considered effective should be reinforced without delay.

3. The coach should use reinforcement appropriately. He should know what rewards and activities are reinforcing to the trainee and should fit reinforcers to the trainee's level of skill, aiming them at higher achievements as learning progresses. The coach should reinforce consistently as the skill is being developed, then reinforce intermittently when skill is fairly well established.

4. The coach should consciously attempt to make these learning developments occur: generalizing and discriminating among situations, and differentiating between supervisory actions which are effective and those which are not.

5. The coach should have numerous contacts with the trainee, planned and unplanned, for scheduling assignments and directing experience and for review and reinforcement. Contacts should not be used in a pedantic or obtrusive way but should indicate progress and difficulties and should prepare the trainee for new assignments.

6. The trainee must be "weaned." He should be given increasing independence to act, but only when successful experience in the earlier stages assures somewhat effective performance. However, the trainee should not be allowed, at any stage, to resort to trial-and-error learning or be kept in the dark on the effectiveness of his action.

Coaching Schedule for the New Supervisor

Below is a schedule of job assignments for coaching the trainee. The topics are described in rather general terms; to ensure adequate coverage of supervisory activities, the coach should be guided by the specific training needs identified earlier—needs which can be subsumed under these general headings.

1. *Teaching "scheduled" job duties* (those which happen frequently and regularly, primarily at daily intervals) as they occur in the job routine:

Placing employees, assigning work, and making assignment changes to get the shift started.

Checking on the condition of machinery and equipment (including preventive maintenance checks).

Checking on production output (following up on schedule).

Paperwork, including keeping time records, recording status changes of employees, helping with outgoing reports, and reviewing incoming reports.

Making housekeeping checks.

Making safety inspections.

Giving induction information to new employees.

Giving training help to new employees.

Following up on progress of new employees through observation and discussion.

In teaching these scheduled activities, the coach will initially demonstrate and explain and have the new supervisor observe on the first day or two. He will then have the new supervisor perform the tasks, starting with the easy or moderately difficult tasks and progressing to the more difficult ones. The new supervisor can begin practicing a number of activities on the same day. He should not be overloaded but should pick up additional activities as he can absorb them. This progressive movement permits the coach to pace the trainee according to his progress and to devote adequate time to modeling the most difficult tasks before having the trainee try his hand at them.

In the practice stage, the coach will use cues and feedback to guide the trainee's execution of each task. The coach will gradually withdraw his help as the trainee's need for it diminishes. The pace of withdrawal will depend on the trainee's progress in mastering the task. At any particular time, coaching may be intensive in some tasks and minimal in others. Generally, the coach will gradually phase out the cues for a task until all are eliminated. Feedback—both for correction of ineffective actions and for reinforcement of effective actions—will be given regularly until performance is satisfactory. Then the coach will reinforce on an intermittent basis. The expectation that intermittent reinforcement will serve to keep an acquired skill going enables the coach to bring efficiency to his coaching chores. Since acquired skills will need attention only now and then, for the sole purpose of reinforcement, the coach can spend more time on stubborn tasks in which skill develops more slowly and can pick up altogether new tasks.

2. *Teaching unscheduled tasks.* When the new supervisor has become competent in the scheduled tasks, the coach will concentrate on unscheduled tasks (some of which the trainee will already have observed):

Taking disciplinary action.

Hearing complaints.

Handling unsafe acts and accidents.

Handling operational problems (quality, efficiency, maintenance, waste, and so forth).

Handling problems of employee performance or behavior.

Overseeing adjustments in machinery or machine settings to achieve changes in production rate or product characteristics.

The trainee will continue to engage in scheduled activities. Gradually, as he takes on unscheduled tasks, he will assume the full range of supervisory duties. Because unscheduled tasks are largely concerned with solving situational problems rather than with executing routine procedures, the coach's job becomes more demanding, requiring an expansion of techniques for modeling and feedback.

As a first step, the coach will handle the problem himself, as an exemplar, but will review the action with the trainee immediately afterward. They will discuss the coach's handling of the situation in these terms:

How was it handled? What was done?

What was effective and what ineffective?

What can the trainee learn from it in the matter of generalizing (applying to other situations of the same sort) or differentiating (applying only to repetitions of the unique circumstances of the specific situation)?

In summary, the coach will try to make each situation he handles during the modeling period a learning experience for the trainee.

After sufficient modeling, the new supervisor will himself deal with unscheduled situations under the coach's surveillance. He may be ready for different kinds of problems at different times. Surveillance will include a preparatory look at the situation, if time permits; direct intervention to prevent an unsuccessful or harmful outcome, by means of cueing and feedback as the action is taking place; and, most important, a review immediately after the action to assess strong and weak aspects of the trainee's performance. Improvement through learning depends on the trainee's knowledge of the specific nature of his weaknesses. But learning depends probably even more on positive feedback—on the trainee's knowledge of being right, with accompanying praise and recognition. It is this kind of feedback that is reinforcing.

The coach will also give the trainee feedback on the anticipated long-term results of his actions, making the connections clear. But the coach will necessarily give immediate feedback of "intermediate" results (which may be a mere prediction of how things will turn out) until the final result is achieved. The success of the coach will depend largely on how well he sizes up the trainee's action as a prediction of ultimate results.

At a later stage, the coach will restrict his efforts to a review of the trainee's handling of the situation, discontinuing direct intervention during the handling.

The intent of coaching, it must be kept in mind, is not to solve the job difficulties for the trainee but to prepare him to confront them successfully himself. Since certain kinds of situations arise infrequently on the job, severely limiting the repetition so important to learning, the coach must make maximum use of them for training purposes when they do occur. His coaching efforts should therefore involve more than the identification of effective and ineffective actions and the reinforcement of the former. The coach should raise the question of the reasons for the effectiveness and ineffectiveness of the trainee's actions in the light of the specific situation addressed. And, looking to the future, he should consciously inquire what the present outcome tells the trainee about circumstances and conditions under which the employed actions are likely to be fruitful. By means of such analyses of difficulties encountered during the coaching period, the new supervisor may be led to examine situations and, through his insight into relationships between the characteristics of a situation and effective responses, to make discriminating use of actions in the future. If we guide him early, he will soon discover that there is a considerable sameness among situations and that certain responses used earlier may fit a number of new problems. Unless he can relate past experience to the solution of current difficulties, the new supervisor will see every situation as new and unprecedented. If the job is therefore an endless series of fresh dilemmas for him, it will not be manageable.

FURTHER CONSIDERATIONS IN MODELING

Successful coaching is not easy. Coaching techniques should take into account not only the lessons of experience but the insights appearing in the psychological literature.*

As indicated earlier, the coach should be an experienced line supervisor at the new supervisor's level of job or higher. If possible, the coach should resemble the trainee in certain important respects. If he is someone the trainee can identify with, the trainee's expectations of success will be increased. ("If he made it, so can I.") But the coach should hold status in the organization; if he is a first-line supervisor, he should command the respect of the hierarchy and be generally regarded as a good supervisor.

In modeling, the coach not only should show what is to be done

---

* As in Bandura, *op. cit.* A number of the considerations discussed in this section are treated in Bandura.

but should demonstrate effectiveness. The trainee should perceive the experience as rewarding to the coach and should see some indication of reinforcement for the coach from the action. The coach should make clear the connection between specific action and its associated results and rewards.

Merely trying to persuade the trainee that such-and-such a course of action will produce results is not adequate coaching, not even in the modeling phase. Success should be evident in the coach's performance, and in the trainee's later application the promised success should come to him as well.

It is simply not good coaching to establish long-range goals for the trainee as the chief or exclusive means of measuring his performance and to allow the issue of effectiveness to remain in midair until all the returns are in. The trainee's performance must be gauged against realistic subgoals and interim standards in order to provide him with the feedback he needs to proceed insightfully with his course of action day by day.

Consistency is essential in coaching. If ultimate performance, as measured against global norms, is not good and contradicts the intermediate indications used by the coach to correct and reinforce the trainee's actions, the coach's actions (and the coach, as well) are likely to be distrusted. If the coach does not practice what he preaches, the resulting confusion will hinder the learning— although the trainee is more likely to be guided by what the coach does than by what he says. Another troublesome inconsistency can arise from differences in modeling between a class instructor dealing with a case and a coach dealing with a similar on-the-job situation. The director of the training program should make sure, through joint consultation on classroom cases, that the case instructor does not use procedures and approaches that differ from those of the coach, although some inconsistency is unavoidable. Finally, the coach can confuse the trainee by giving reinforcement inconsistently. Not knowing what type of behavior will gain approval from the coach, the trainee may develop a repertoire of superstitious actions established by incidental reinforcement.

The trainee should be aware of the connection between rewards and actions. Although some learning may occur without such awareness, it is hard to conceive of efficiency in learning the supervisory job if the trainee is not conscious of the connection. Indeed, in such a case it would be difficult to establish a convincing rationale, through reinforcement, for the repetition of human acts. A major task of the instructor is to make sure that the trainee knows that certain rewards are dependent on certain acts.

As performance is being shaped, the coach will require increasingly higher levels of skill for reinforcement. The ultimate objective is to set high standards of performance as a basis for rewards, avoiding noncontingent rewards, so that the trainee will have a high-quality performance norm when he goes on his own and must depend in large measure on self-reinforcement. His self-esteem should prevent him from rewarding himself with self-satisfaction or other available self-reinforcers for performance below the norm.

The supervisor's job involves learning a series of competencies. The supervisor must develop skill in his various functions by means of activities. Some of the functions hold more interest for the trainee than others. Only the rare trainee has a substantial beginning interest in all parts of the supervisory job. The coach's problem—and a challenging one, with few answers—is to bring about consistently good performance in all functions of the supervisor's job even when such differences in interest exist. For low-interest functions, one answer may be to provide sufficient external reinforcement to elicit successful performance and, with it, the intrinsic satisfaction that accompanies success. A possible by-product is the awakening of interest in the activity itself. But without such development, the chief hope lies in bringing about successful performance and whatever intrinsically rewarding experience resides in it and at the same time leading the trainee, through judicious contingent use of extrinsic rewards, to the establishment of high standards for self-evaluation of performance. These may stand more firmly if the generalized effect from training in other tasks takes hold.

Generalization of two kinds may occur. First, since it is not practical to model actions related to every conceivable situation the new supervisor will encounter (it is difficult enough to model the full run of major problems occurring at irregular intervals), some measure of generalization in terms of transferable principles, rules, and procedures is needed in order to bring comprehensive training within reach. No supervisory problem is ever exactly reproduced. The coach must provide the trainee with modeling and guidance in enough situations to enable him to develop generalized rules of action that would apply to situations not yet encountered.

Economy of training is at issue. Obviously, verbal instruction by the coach is helpful; coaching is not a dumb show. In the classroom, although each supervisor's direct experience with cases as a role player or discussion participant is essential, modeling and verbal instruction can be used to move supervisors through a quick succession of case situations and condensed versions of others, to maximize the effect of practice when it occurs, and to provide opportunities for insight into effective kinds of actions. Thus the process of evolving and identifying rules of wide applicability is expedited.

Second, generalization can apparently occur in the trainee's expectations of success. If the new supervisor experiences success in some activities, he may generalize his expectations of effective performance to others, heightening his overall sense of efficacy. Strong confidence in his powers to succeed can significantly influence his learning of later tasks and help him withstand certain inevitable failures without loss of motivation. The lesson for the coach, therefore, is to help the trainee realize achievement early in his training, with the hope that success will feed upon success. The trainee himself should directly experience the accomplishments.

As with all matters, there are limitations. Not every successful experience will lead to an increase in expectations, nor will all individuals react to an experience in the same way. A person's past history of successes and failures is a predisposing influence on expectations.

CHAPTER 6

Measuring Performance

M OVING the new supervisor through the early stages of training is perhaps easier than improving or sustaining his performance once he has acquired some competency. Our knowledge
of how to effect this later development is limited. Yet experience
with it and budding research point to a number of germane factors.
One of the most important is the measurement of performance and
setting of goals, which we will examine in this chapter. Two other
significant factors—the maintenance of motivation and additional
training to meet situational needs—will be covered in the chapters
following.

Unfortunately, it is virtually impossible to discuss performance
measurement and related standards without discussing management by objectives (MBO), management by results, management
by objectives and results—or whatever the popular system is called
at the moment by the particular advocate. Of course, performance
measurement as a management tool antedates MBO by many dec-
ades, but MBO has somehow assumed title to it and it is rarely
discussed outside that context. So, to stay in step, we will examine
MBO, critically and in some detail, even though it will carry us into

concepts—participation, for one—that might be more pertinent in some other context.

First we will look at what experience and research conducted outside the context of MBO tell us about such major components as emphasis on results, performance measures and goal setting, and participation. Then we will examine findings from research focused on MBO itself. Finally, we will attempt to draw practical conclusions to guide the operating manager in improving and evaluating the performance of his subordinates, particularly the novice supervisor.

A Look at Elements of MBO

The operating executive's problem with MBO is how to make it work and keep it working. In the beginning, he may not see this as a problem of any size; he may be dazzled by MBO's almost irresistible appeal. Who can argue convincingly against a system of management that specifies responsibilities and the indexes by which performance of these responsibilities is to be measured; that sets participative goals on these indexes; and that requires periodic reviews of progress toward the goals?

The magic words in the MBO formula—"results" and "participation" and "goal setting" chief among them—are the clincher for the operating executive, who does not have time to find out precisely what behavioral science has to teach but wants to avoid appearing unlettered and unprogressive. Consequently, he plunges into MBO with a blind faith and a naive idea of what it takes to make it work, convinced that any system so logically constructed and vouched for by a good segment of the academic community must be effective. The system's appeal thus assured, the manager is likely to make a second assumption: that it can be readily adapted to his organization.

Simple prudence dictates a cautious and questioning approach to MBO. Much is known about participation and goal setting; they have been the subject of considerable research, observation, and hypothesizing. A cursory look will reveal that participation has worked well in some situations, less so in others; well with some individuals, less so with others. Certain conclusions about goal setting are equally clear: that the level of the goal is related to achievment experience and to temperamental and motivational characteristics of individuals. These indications, though not uncovered in an MBO setting, must surely have relevance for the MBO program and its application.

EMPHASIS ON RESULTS

Perhaps the ascendant word in the MBO glossary is "results," which has a strong built-in appeal for operating managers, who are unremittingly preoccupied with "bottom line" figures. Although not enough research has been done on how an emphasis on results affects performance, such emphasis appears to make practical sense. Yet our experience would lead us to raise questions about the kinds of results we are striving for (how important, how relevant) and perhaps to observe restraint in emphasizing them. The possible effects of focusing on results as the criterion of managerial effectiveness need to be given thoughtful consideration.* Two possible adverse effects in our effort to develop new supervisors are (1) inadequate attention to means and (2) inadequate feedback from actions taken to bring about the learning that is needed to repeat successful results.

RESEARCH ON GOAL SETTING

Much of the research on goal setting has dealt with levels of aspiration. The findings point to the influence on levels of aspiration of such factors as personality variables, previous successes and failures, group standards and social pressures, and an intellectual component affecting judgment.

Personality variables seem to exert an especially strong effect on goal setting, and the achievement motive is particularly germane. The hypothesis that achievement-motivated people (those in whom the motive to achieve success is stronger than the motive to avoid failure) choose tasks of intermediate difficulty has been amply confirmed by research findings.† People motivated to avoid failure

---

* See Campbell et al., *op. cit.*, pp. 451–457, for a critical discussion of this issue.
† See John W. Atkinson and Norman T. Feathers, eds., *A Theory of Achievement Motivation* (New York: John Wiley & Sons, 1966), pp. 91, 148.

tend to select either easy or difficult tasks, in which the probability of success is great or small. The reaction to success or failure also tends to differ between those with strong motivation to achieve and those fearful of failure. Atypical shifts in levels of aspiration, seemingly irrational, occur more frequently among the latter.* The reaction is also related to the difficulty or easiness of the task in which the success or failure is experienced.

The most important conclusion to be drawn from the research is the simplest one: goal setting is a highly individual process.

RESEARCH ON PARTICIPATION

Much of the research on participation has focused on the relative merits of supervisory styles—person-oriented versus work-oriented. Stogdill surveyed a wide range of person-oriented behaviors (democratic, permissive, follower-oriented, participative, and considerate) and work-oriented behaviors (autocratic, restrictive, task-oriented, socially distant, directive, and structured) to determine their relationship to productivity, satisfaction, and group cohesiveness. The findings which emerged were these, in broad summary:

All the person-oriented styles tend to be positively related to follower satisfaction, and some (freedom of member participation in group activities and concern for followers' welfare and comfort) to group cohesiveness. But person-oriented behaviors are not consistently related to productivity.

Only those work-oriented behaviors that "maintain role differentiation and let followers know what to expect" have a consistent positive relationship to productivity. And the structuring of member expectations appears to have a broad efficacy; it has a favorable relationship, alone among the work-oriented patterns, to follower satisfaction and group cohesiveness.†

The fit of participation to the type of leader and to characteristics of followers is an important consideration. Although they indicated the need for more research, Fiedler and Chemers came to this conclusion: "It is obvious, however, that the simple prescription of

* Atkinson and Feathers, *op. cit.,* pp. 25–27, 154.

† Ralph M. Stogdill, *Handbook of Leadership: A Survey of Theory and Research* (New York: The Free Press, 1974), p. 419.

'participative management for better performance' cannot be taken
without serious qualifications. It should be used only for
relationship-motivated leaders and only in groups in which the participants in the decision-making processes are of comparatively
high intelligence or especially knowledgeable." *

The compatibility of leader characteristics and follower characteristics appears to be a primary influence on leader effectiveness.
Employees tend to perform or respond better and more comfortably under supervisors whose personalities are compatible with
their own—the nonauthoritarian and independent employees
under participative supervisors, the authoritarian and less independent employees under nonparticipative and directive leaders. In
short, task-oriented employees generally perform better under
task-oriented supervisors, and person-oriented employees under
person-oriented supervisors.†

Compatibility appears to extend beyond personalities to aspects
of the situation—particularly to task structure and work-group
structure. The broadened compatibility combinations appear to be
(1) task-oriented employees, task-oriented supervisor, high task
structure, and large, structured groups, and (2) person-oriented
employees, person-oriented supervisor, low or medium task structure, and small, less highly structured groups.

Defining the situation to include leader–member relations, task
structure, and position power, Fiedler and Chemers concluded
from their investigations that task-centered leadership was more
effective than employee-centered leadership in situations that were
very favorable or very unfavorable for the leader, but employee-
centered leadership was more effective in moderately favorable
situations.‡

While much remains to be learned about participative leadership,
enough evidence exists at this point to suggest that participation,
though often effective, is not universally so and must be viewed in
the light of its appropriateness for the supervisor, the subordinate,

* Fred E. Fiedler and Martin M. Chemers, *Leadership and Effective Management*
(Glenview, Ill.: Scott, Foresman and Company, 1974), pp. 112–113.

† See Campbell, *op. cit.,* p. 422, and Stogdill, *op. cit.,* pp. 111, 359, for statements
on leader-follower compatibility.

‡ Fiedler and Chemers, *op. cit.,* pp. 73–91.

and the situation (nature and structure of the job and other factors), and in the light of outcomes of importance to the organization.

For discriminative use of participation in decision making, Vroom's decision-process model has much to recommend it as a tentative guide. Research on the model is not yet conclusive, but many managers will see logic and experience as support for its use. The Vroom model provides a means of diagnosing a problem in terms of its attributes and determining an appropriate decision-making approach. A series of questions is raised about the problem (regarding the quality of the solution required, the amount of information possessed by manager and subordinates, acceptance of the decision by subordinates, extent of structure in the problem, sharing of organizational goals, and likelihood of conflict among subordinates). The answers to the questions identify the attributes of the problem and point to the optimal decision-making process or processes for it—ranging by degree from independent solutions to delegation of the problem, if it is an individual one, to the subordinate for solution. Underlying the model is a set of rules protecting both the quality and acceptance of the decision.*

In regard to the discriminative use of participation, it is also helpful to keep in mind the possibly reinforcing characteristics of participation and the role of contingency in reinforcement. Participation could be made contingent upon good job performance.† Employees whose performance was poor or who did not improve would not be permitted to participate in decisions or to participate to the same extent. Thus participation would be selective rather than a categorical prescription applied to all employees.

The appropriateness of participation to both personality and

* Victor H. Vroom and Philip W. Yetton, *Leadership and Decision-Making* (Pittsburgh: University of Pittsburgh Press, 1973), p. 194. Major ingredients of the model (decision methods, problem attribute questions, the related decision-process flowchart, and underlying rules), most of which are referred to above, are contained in pages 13, 32–58, 182–196, and 218–220; but the entire volume deals with various aspects of the model and related research. An abbreviated description of the model is given in Victor H. Vroom, "Leadership Revisited," in Eugene L. Cass and Frederick G. Zimmer, eds., *Man and Work in Society* (New York: Van Nostrand Reinhold Company, 1975), pp. 220–234.

† Thomas K. Connellan, *How to Improve Human Performance: Behaviorism in Business and Industry* (New York: Harper & Row, 1978), pp. 132–133.

situation does not ensure its effectiveness. A key question is: Effectiveness in what terms? Participation is more likely to be reflected in increased satisfaction than in increased productivity. Another consideration is the manager's skill in carrying out the participative approach.

Research on MBO Itself

Operating managers, occupied with other matters, may be excused for failing to make a critical review of the research findings on underlying components of MBO. But it is inexcusable to espouse MBO without reviewing the findings now available on MBO programs themselves or attempt to install an MBO program without the guiding knowledge, now available in the literature, of the experience of other companies.

The findings from studies of MBO programs are mixed but substantially positive. The programs were found to have advantages and disadvantages, the latter rising, apparently, from poor execution. The general appraisal of the system and attitudes toward it remain favorable, not only because of the successful experience but also, perhaps, because it is so easy to attribute lack of success to poor execution or poor managers. Since it is unrealistic to expect perfect application by human beings, we may never know whether MBO is valid in its pristine concepts. It is evident, however, that distinct problems of execution must be avoided or overcome if the system's full potential is to be realized.

Raia, who finds merit in MBO and whose recent book is a useful guide for MBO practitioners, discusses a number of practical problems encountered in its implementation: lack of top management involvement and support, distortion in management philosophy, difficulty of setting objectives, overemphasis on objectives, increased paperwork, increased time pressures, lack of relevant skills, lack of individual motivation, poor integration with other systems, and inappropriate strategy for change.*

In their review of research studies of MBO programs, Carroll

---

* Anthony P. Raia, *Managing by Objectives* (Glenview, Ill.: Scott, Foresman and Company, 1974), pp. 148–171. The terminology is taken from Raia's problem headings.

and Tosi reported a number of favorable changes in performance and behavior: better planning, greater satisfaction with the basis for performance measurement, positive attitudes toward the work situation, and increased task-oriented communication between superior and subordinate. Negative effects were also found, possibly arising from misapplication, in connection with extensive paperwork, difficulties in measuring performance and setting goals in nonquantifiable areas of responsibility, questionable accuracy of data reported, organizational instability, and problems of fitting the system into the organizational setting.*

Carroll and Tosi conducted their own studies of an MBO program in an industrial firm, using questionnaires and interviews. Their findings are highly instructive for any manager faced with the task of implementing an MBO program.† The questionnaire study revealed the importance of such factors as clarity and relevance of goals, frequency of feedback, personality of the subordinate, and characteristics of the superior. Among the findings from the interview study were these: the manager's need to see benefits to himself in the program, the importance of high-level commitment, the need for adequate performance reviews, and the relation of organizational constraints to the degree of influence over goals. Interestingly, the questionnaire study found that subordinate participation in goal setting did not have a favorable effect on goal success, expenditure of effort, or relationships with superior. But there were indications that participation is more likely to have an impact if it involves more than goal setting and is part of a general managerial style.

THE QUESTION OF REWARDS FOR PERFORMANCE

The issue of rewarding performance has perhaps received too little attention in the MBO literature. Referring to an MBO study which, on follow-up, uncovered complaints of inadequate incentive, Luthans and Kreitner perceived the missing ingredient to be a "systematic program of positive consequences for making MBO

* Stephen J. Carroll, Jr., and Henry L. Tosi, Jr., *Management by Objectives: Applications and Research* (New York: Macmillan Publishing Company, 1973), pp. 14–15.
† See Carroll and Tosi, *op. cit.*, pp. 40–45, for a detailed discussion.

work and for achieving stated objectives." In this regard they see benefits in combining MBO with organizational behavior modification. And they propose reinforcement for approximating objectives between the process of setting objectives at the beginning and appraising by results at the end.*

Cummings and Schwab see difficulties in attaching rewards equitably to MBO goals because of the individualized nature of the goals and the key role played by the subordinate in the evaluation process. A direct tie-in, they feel, may encourage the subordinate to subvert both goal setting and performance review.†

Where It All Leads

These research findings as well as experience and good sense suggest that the operating manager has a number of lessons to apply if he is to ensure reasonable success in installing and maintaining an MBO program. First of all, he must recognize that an MBO program cannot stand well in isolation; it must be integrated into the managerial system of the company. Moreover, the program will be hard put to function exclusively at certain levels; it should have support from higher levels and be used up and down the line. If an organization is unlikely to accept MBO as a way of managing and will not take the implant because of incompatible philosophy and rigid practice, a companywide effort at full implementation is probably unjustified—although limited aspects of the MBO program may work in pockets of the organization.

Even if the organization and the time are right for MBO, the program will not work without training. It is not enough simply to search for objective measures of performance, brush lightly against problem-solving techniques as the means of improving job performance, and role-play a goal-setting session and a performance review session. Evaluative and interpersonal skills need maximum attention if they are to develop. In addition, the superior's coaching

---

* Fred Luthans and Robert Kreitner, *Organizational Behavior Modification* (Glenview, Ill.: Scott, Foresman and Company, 1975), p. 194.

† L. L. Cummings and Donald P. Schwab, *Performance in Organizations: Determinants and Appraisal* (Glenview, Ill.: Scott, Foresman and Company, 1973), p. 96.

skills may need sharpening if the subordinate is to improve his performance and achieve his goals. The effectiveness of the system depends not only on the soundness of its parts but on their skillful execution. To make MBO work, managers need a high level of skill and a large body of conceptual knowledge involving goal setting, participation, performance review, feedback, and reinforcement. Thus the training required for installing and maintaining an MBO program is formidable indeed. Many managers already possess pertinent skills and knowledge, but rarely to the degree required for undertaking an MBO program.

GOALS AND INDEXES

A few major questions need to be settled in regard to goals: Goals in what? Measured by what? At what level? How many?

Obviously, it would be impractical to set goals in the absence of gauges. Some indexes of performance are required, and they must (1) cover significant aspects of job performance, (2) measure objectives that demonstrably serve the interests of the company, and (3) truly reflect the employee's performance. This last requirement is crucial; if the index does not reflect what the employee does or does not do, there is no purpose in setting goals for him on it. Thus control is essential.

The indexes usually associated with the supervisory job are somewhat suspect on this score. An enterprising staff organization will devise a truly amazing array of indexes for measuring the effectiveness of operating departments and, indirectly at least, the effectiveness of line managers and supervisors. There are usually efficiency reports, output reports, downtime reports, labor cost reports, supply cost reports, waste reports, quality reports (percentage of offgrade goods, volume of returned goods), accident incidence reports, Workers' Compensation cost reports, turnover reports, absenteeism reports, and on and on. The first-line supervisor is literally deluged with reports. But the issue is: Will they serve as valid indicators of the effectiveness of *his* performance, even assuming that they are pertinent to important organizational objectives?

In many cases they will not. These reports usually reflect results from the department as a whole, not from the section or shift under the jurisdiction of the supervisor. His input goes into the mix but is not compelling. The index is more appropriate for the department head. For measuring the supervisor's performance, the index should, in effect, be coterminous with the scope of his job or at least not extend far beyond it. Such limited operational reports exist in few companies, primarily because it is impossible or uneconomical to collect data restricted to subunits of the manufacturing operation or to break down global figures accurately enough to specify the contribution of each supervisor's operating area.

The problem of control may exist even when the report is restricted to the supervisor's area of assignment or when the data emanate exclusively from his processes. Turnover tends to fluctuate with community labor market trends and is influenced by other factors which the supervisor is powerless to control. Quality is often affected in a fugitive way by prior processes. The causes of accident frequency, to cite another index, are often an unresolved mystery; accident incidence seems at times to operate independently of what supervisors do.

In addition, on all indexes the element of chance comes into play, accounting for minor fluctuations that a supervisor can do absolutely nothing to eliminate. Yet these insignificant shifts on the scale are often interpreted as evidence of improved or worsened performance by the supervisor.

A desirable though not always obtainable feature of an index is objectivity—by which we usually mean capable of being subject to impersonal arithmetic count. Without units of measurement, it is obviously difficult to specify how far we want to go and to know whether we have arrived. However, devising valid indexes that quantify all the important supervisory functions is an extremely troublesome and challenging task. In addition, in our drive for objectivity we may design a set of indexes that will give a partial and lopsided measurement of overall job performance and that overstate outcomes to which the company assigns little worth. Overemphasis on objectivity may also lead us to assign numerical values to basically subjective indexes, under the delusion that they are thus made objective. Or perhaps worst of all, it may lead us to dismiss subjective measures as untrustworthy or unessential in appraising supervisory performance. Informed judgment has its uses, as we shall see.

If the manager were concerned only with measuring his subordinate's performance and setting goals, valid and objective indexes (assuming they were available or could be developed) would meet his full need. But the manager must go beyond finding out where the supervisor stands and designating a higher goal. He must be concerned with how the supervisor is to move from where he is to where he wants to be—from point A to point B on the index.

Inescapably, learning is at the heart of this process. We can reasonably assume that what the supervisor has already learned (his present skill) is being employed to peg him at his current level on the performance indexes. In order for him to reach a higher level, he must obviously perform new activities effectively or improve his performance of the old. How? He is already doing what he knows how to do.

Problem solving is not likely to be extremely helpful to him. Problem-solving models designed to spot sources of trouble in subpar operations or performance may not be readily adaptable to operations that are in relatively good shape but that could be improved further. And if the problem-solving approach did put a finger on factors whose improvement would raise the supervisor's mark on the index, what would he do about it?

Obviously, the supervisor needs training help, which can best be given through coaching by the superior. We recognize such need in our efforts to improve the performance of new supervisors; old and experienced supervisors faced with the challenge of doing better than they can currently do have a similar need. Inevitably, if the manager is to aid the supervisor's performance, he must relegate the operational indexes to a lesser role and move closer to the supervisor's actions, focusing on more immediate feedback on how things are going.

In order for feedback to work, it must follow closely upon actions to signal effectiveness or ineffectiveness. Obviously, this is a requirement which a delayed operational report, issued at weekly intervals, does not fulfill; it does not discriminate among actions. If the employee shows up well in the index, he tends to be reinforced in whatever he has done (or done recently), the good and bad alike. If, on the other hand, he shows up poorly on the scale, there is no indication of what brought him down. Were all aspects of his performance bad? If not, which were good and which were bad? The index does not inform him.

If the feedback is immediate, it will indicate which activities went right and which went wrong. The right actions can then be reinforced. But in order to provide maximum aid in improving poor performance, the feedback must be specific about the weaknesses, diagnostically pinpointing the exact nature of the trouble. To achieve this end, an agent is needed early in the feedback process, a coaching superior who appraises performance, without delay, on largely subjective bases, reinforcing some things and assisting in the reshaping of others. And he should unabashedly deal with activities and means.

To summarize, in order to improve the supervisor's performance, we should move close to him with measures of performance that are specific and immediate and that will give information needed for coaching him. We must be concerned with how well he carries out specific activities. In the final analysis, such indications can arise only from professional judgment. The coach (or superior serving as coach) examines the immediate effect of the supervisor's action, and indeed the action itself in process, and makes a judgment on those aspects of the activity that made it effective. This judgment should be communicated explicitly to the supervisor—accompanied by an expression of approval and other available reinforcers—so that the reinforcement is tied in no uncertain terms to the specific activity.

The judgment must be an informed one. It should derive authentically from the coach's training and from experiential evidence that the immediate action he is reinforcing will ultimately lead to improvements on the valid larger and delayed indexes. Confirmation is all-important. Unless the new supervisor ultimately sees results on the indexes, the effectiveness of the trainer will be impaired and the trainee will suffer from inconsistent feedback. But the coach cannot wait for ultimate returns. He must be a professional, and as a professional he must size up actions and interim results as of now and make, in effect, an informed prediction of eventual results.

In his coaching, the trainer should be concerned not only with teaching effective actions but with inculcating the professional standards that provide a sound basis for evaluating activities. A department head is indeed fortunate if his supervisors are expert enough in their field and well enough equipped with performance standards to provide their own immediate feedback and mature enough to be sustained by it until the larger and more remote returns come in. But this is a long-range development. With new supervisors (and experienced ones whose performance must be improved), the coach must provide immediate feedback, including reinforcement as a primary element, using reinforcers in a clearly contingent manner so that the trainee can ultimately reinforce himself by carrying out activities in such a way as to meet the inculcated standards of performance.

Level of Goals. Goals should be set realistically, with due regard to the personality of the supervisor, his prior successes, and other variables identified in the research on goal setting. Obviously, a goal should not be set in isolation from the supervisor's means of getting there. Are the resources available to him? Does he have the required skill? Will attainment of the goal require better execution of current activities or learning new activities? What help are we prepared to give him? Unless we take these considerations into account, goal setting will be an exercise in futility and an invitation to frustration. We cannot leave these matters to the new supervisor, in effect consigning him to thrash about in trial-and-error efforts. The appropriate level of a goal for an inexperienced supervisor will bear a direct relationship to the amount of help we are prepared to give him in regard to means. And if he is to learn anything useful for the future, a major part of that help should involve conscious coaching. Experienced supervisors striving to improve performance are likely to have the same need.

It should be kept in mind that most operational indexes are based on standards derived from machine studies, output records, and historical data of various sorts. Such standards are usually set on rather solid information, carefully developed by accountants and industrial engineers, and usually represent a level that ensures satis-factory profit to the company. Unless conditions change to invali-date such standards, there would seem to be no reason to revise them. Yet MBO practitioners rarely appear content with retaining current standards as goals and with using them as points of refer-ence in reviewing performance. The movement is ever onward and upward, and the higher goals are often the airy product of mere aspiration, externally induced.

The MBO practitioner may attempt to draw distinctions among goals on the basis of attainability and desirability; but the whole exercise of goal setting for an individual supervisor would be more convincing if the process gave prominence to means—indeed, if it examined the means thoroughly before specifying the exact goal, so that the supervisor could realistically size up his chance of improv-ing his mark on the index—and by how far—before the commit-ment was made. In many instances the supervisor, without inves-tigating means, responds with fanciful aspiration. And to make his dreams come true we give him a quick course in problem solving.

Number of Goals. How many goals are needed? Goals should be set for important responsibilities of the job and not simply attached to objective indexes that may be easy to come by but that represent minor or irrelevant matters. And, as experience rather than re-search teaches us, the goals should not be conflicting—for example, goals for a high level of efficiency and quality in combination which, by the nature of the particular manufacturing process, may be unat-tainable because they have a negative influence on each other.

Common sense would suggest limiting goals to a manageable number, but relative emphasis and the scheduling of reinforcement may be more important than absolute numbers. Certainly we should not neglect any significant responsibility of the job and should strive to improve performance or to continue effective per-formance overall. But priorities are in order. We can resolve the matter by establishing our primary goals in major responsibilities or in those aspects of the job that are currently most troublesome.

To strive for dramatic improvement in an index, period after period, is naive. We expect improvement to occur in needed areas but we should also expect the rate of improvement to slacken or cease altogether, despite our efforts, when a relatively high level of performance has been reached. Thus we need to focus strongly on some goals to achieve large improvements and less strongly on others to keep moving forward or to hold our position. The mix will tend to vary from time to time.

Fortunately, the principles underlying the scheduling of reinforcement come to our aid. In moving the supervisor into new or intensified activities to achieve certain objectives, we need to reinforce effective actions frequently and consistently. After the behaviors have been established, intermittent reinforcement will help sustain them. Thus activities tied to the period's primary goals can be reinforced heavily and often, while already established behaviors related to other goals need be reinforced only intermittently. In this way, goal setting and reinforcement can be made a manageable process for the superior. Of course, the schedule of reinforcement alone does not guarantee that the behavior will be sustained; the nature of the reinforcer is of crucial importance, as we shall see. But the combination of a cogent reinforcer and an intermittent schedule is a strong tool for sustaining behavior.

A Practical View of Participation

Several cautions should be observed in the matter of participation. To begin with, in using it we should take into account the subordinate's personal characteristics and his job situation.* To allow a fearful or naive subordinate to participate extensively in goal setting is questionable. Moreover, a disorganized job structure with uncertain boundaries may require more of a directive than participative approach. In addition, participation in goal setting may not be very fruitful unless it is done in the framework of a broad participation in decisions affecting the job. The subordinate may be

---

* This discussion focuses primarily on individual participation. For a discussion of group participation in decision making, see Campbell et al., *op. cit.,* pp. 428–441. Campbell and his co-authors note a number of pertinent issues (p.440), including "the effects of ambiguous group boundaries, an organizational value system which seems to value reaching a consensus quickly (independently of so-called conformity behavior), the tendency for group decisions to be 'riskier' than individual decisions, and the manager's problems in maintaining subordinate individuality under conditions of group participation."

hard put to function efficiently with some doors open and some closed or with an uncertain knowledge of which ones are open and which are closed.

The superior needs to keep his purposes firmly in mind. If he is interested primarily in improving the subordinate's satisfaction, participation is indicated. But if he is concerned with achieving results that are economically advantageous to the organization—as well as with providing the subordinate with a rewarding experience—uncircumscribed reliance on participation may not be the way. In such a case, purposes can conflict and can produce a participative process and an imposed solution—and a disillusioned subordinate. A still worse procedure is to create the appearance of participation so as to maneuver the subordinate into "discovering" the superior's predetermined solution.

The assumption that goal setting is motive enough for goal attainment is not well founded. Similarly, we would be foolish to assume that the attainment of goals is a sufficient reward or will serve as a motivator for sustained or increased effort. It may well be, as we will see later, that increases in levels of aspiration are required to sustain motivation when goals are reached, or that other reinforcers must be brought into play.

If we accept the thesis that the motivational effect of the goal-setting process lies in the subordinate's commitment to the goal, we are still faced with the problem of finding the means for securing such commitment. The answer may not be as simple as we have supposed. Participation is popularly viewed, with considerable justification, as the most effective means of ensuring commitment; yet the pitfalls of participation must temper our expectations. Participation will not work with all subordinates or with all kinds of goals. Nor, to go a step further, will motivation provide the complete answer to goal attainment, even if the subordinate's commitment is obtained through participation or other means.

A COACHING APPROACH RELATED TO MEANS

We know that frequent feedback is needed for improvement of performance, and we may use feedback to apply such reinforcers as information on effective actions and expressions of approval. But the value of frequent feedback, as distinct from periodic reviews, points to the importance of coaching—with reinforcement—to move the subordinate toward the goal. If the subordinate lacks the skill or knowledge to reach the goal, participative goal setting will not give him the help he needs. The superior must provide whatever coaching is necessary, with specific and immediate feedback. Such feedback is at the heart of our training effort with new supervisors. Frequent contacts are essential for adequate coaching. Moreover, coaching should not focus solely on activities related to MBO goals (though attention should be paid to them). It should also be concerned with total job performance and with a balance among the parts—whether we are in a position to measure them objectively or not or have goals for them or not. Otherwise, the subordinate's efforts will be expended in narrow channels, to the detriment of the larger functions of the job.

Even with major, legitimate goals, the coaching superior must make a professionally based distinction between activities that are related to ultimate results and activities that have a limited and temporary effect and that may result in neglect of other approaches with greater potential utility. As a subordinate moves toward a goal, there are certain activities he should continue to do, certain ones he should drop or modify, and certain new ones he should adopt. The progressive nature of his undertaking and the changing nature of the situation argue for a flexible attack involving frequent soundings and revisions of tactics when necessary.

Coaching will necessarily focus on activities rather than results—despite the disdain for activities shown by some MBO advocates. The superior must provide guidance in activities until results are genuinely achieved and must rely on judgment to ensure that the activities make a significant contribution toward the goal.

THE FIT OF MBO TO MAJOR RESPONSIBILITIES

The attempt to adapt MBO to traditional major responsibilities is a legitimate cause for concern. Difficulties can arise, for example, if a goal is set in a major endeavor (such as efficiency or quality) that has traditionally been the subject of accounting reports; that is gauged by standards already established and repeatedly updated by industrial engineers or quality control technicians; and that has been the target of an extensive and unrelenting battery of managerial techniques and programs—that is, indeed, the organization's very reason for existence. At first blush, an MBO program appears an easy fit, since the critical measurement tools are already in place, and MBO could merely add precision and formality to goal setting and performance review. But what about the means of improving performance? How are we to do better in a responsibility that has already commanded our full attention and our best efforts in developing activities, procedures, and programs? Where do we go from here?

When we have already worked energetically on quality or efficiency, our new response in the face of a higher goal may be to foist the burden on someone else ("tightening the screws" on the employees is a popular gambit) or to move into left field in search of unique solutions which the organization will not accept and cannot be made to accept. In the first instance, the effort may run afoul of another important organizational objective—maintaining a stable workforce, for example—and may in itself be counterproductive, since the response to pressure tactics or buck passing is likely to be negative or, at best, unpredictable. In the latter instance, the action will probably be disruptive as it bangs against established and successful practices; it is also likely to be nonproductive, since an unacceptable decision has small chance of success.

The merit in "ordinary" means should not be overlooked. If we propose new and untried approaches to a goal, the supervisor may neglect the means at hand in the daily routine of his job. It is through improvement in day-to-day activities, involving organization of the job and execution of the routine, that individual progress and departmental progress are likely to be realized. It is difficult to see how attaining goals that are pertinently tied to such job responsibilities as efficiency and quality can be divorced from improving performance in the commonplace. Innovative means would be more heavily required (along with closer coaching) if we added or changed the supervisor's responsibilities or functions—a change which should not occur solely because of wayward goal setting.

Of course, large goals are useful, and we should review the global situation throughout the year. But such a review does not obviate the need for attention to the parade of activities that take a supervisor through the days of the week and give close-in indications of progress. Routine activities comprise the "guts" of a department's ongoing work, especially in stable periods. A search for better routes to the goal is not to be discouraged, but we should not ignore the possibility of better movement along the established route through improvements in the daily activities of the job.

Is MBO for Everyone?

Is MBO useful for improving performance in the case of all managers?

The MBO research appears to support the idea of higher performance levels through MBO, in comparison with other management approaches not involving goal setting, feedback on performance related to goals, and subordinate participation in goal setting.* Of these three aspects of MBO, possibly stronger cases can be made for goal setting and feedback (if it is frequent enough) than for participation in goal setting.

Personal characteristics appear to be a compelling factor in the success or failure of MBO. Evidence suggests that those who are already good managers are more likely to carry out MBO effectively. The response to difficult goals appears to depend on the manager's confidence and maturity. Managers who are highly motivated to succeed and those fearful of failure are likely to choose different levels of goals—and to have different reactions to success or failure. The achievement motive appears to be related to feedback as well as goals. Managers high on achievement tend to be interested in concrete feedback on concrete goals, as clear measures of how they are progressing.†

We should also realize that MBO can change the work situation (the superior subordinate relationship notably). In so doing, it may create short-range problems of adjustment or possibly, if basic per-

* Carroll and Tosi, *op. cit.,* p. 16.
† David C. McClelland and Robert S. Steele, *Human Motivation: A Book of Readings* (Morristown, N.J.: General Learning Press, 1973), p. 500.

sonality and motivational factors are strongly at odds with the new requirements, insurmountable problems of adjustment.

Perhaps the essence of MBO, judging by its effect, is that it helps to structure the job. This purpose alone may be useful for many employees, particularly new supervisors. Obviously, goal setting does give better (even if limited) direction to the supervisor's efforts than the general admonition to improve. But we must wonder about MBO's utility in jobs that do not need further structuring and for supervisors who do not need their jobs structured. And a larger question persists: When we need structuring or whatever other advantages MBO can provide, must we take the MBO panoply, with all its trappings?

If we undertake the larger MBO objectives, we should at least do so with our eyes open, keeping in mind the experiences of other people and the findings from research. We should give thought, for example, to this conclusion of Carroll and Tosi from their intensive study of an MBO program: "An important finding of this research is that MBO affects different managers in different ways. The results obtained indicate that in many respects MBO should be tailored to the individual and his position rather than being presented as a single, defined approach for all managers." *

* Carroll and Tosi, *op. cit.*, p. 45.

CHAPTER 7

Sustaining Motivation

A SSUMING that the job is manageable and the subordinate is reasonably competent in it, the issue of performance often boils down to one of motivation. How can the superior keep the subordinate's motivation alive as a force for sustained or improved performance? Discussion of this question is germane to our further development of the new supervisor and to the supervisor's own efforts to sustain the performance of his employees.

Instead of reaching for the nostrum of the day in despair and frustration, the superior should review the state of the art. As he does, he will begin to realize the complexities arising from differences in individual responses to the reinforcers that are intended to move performance along. A number of issues are involved here, including the nature and strength of reinforcers, satiety and loss of potency in reinforcers, levels of aspiration, maturity, and self-regulation. Yet if the superior combines research and related indications with the lessons of experience, he may uncover a useful premise or two that will support action. At the least, he should emerge with a healthy skepticism that will prevent him from taking foolish action.

Critical Research Questions

Research on sustaining motivation has focused (though still inconclusively) on a number of critical questions.

1. *Can the probably negative effect of satisfaction on motivation be overridden by a heightened goal aspiration? When a goal is achieved and satisfaction experienced, will a subordinate "go for more"?*

The answer, it might be maintained with some justification, will depend upon whether the reward is extrinsic or intrinsic. Intrinsic rewards are essentially self-rewards (such as the feeling of personal achievement), and occur immediately. Extrinsic rewards are given by the organization and are usually delayed. Research suggests that satisfaction with an extrinsic reward is likely to decrease goal aspirations, while satisfaction with an intrinsic reward is likely to increase them.

The key to heightened aspirations may lie not in the distinction between intrinsic and extrinsic rewards but in the value of the reward, however we classify it, for the individual. Distinctions may indeed be largely semantic in this light. It takes temerity to vouch for the "internal" response of the individual. Promotion is obviously an extrinsic reinforcer in the sense of being administered by the organization; yet internal satisfaction and a sense of personal achievement certainly can accompany it. Pay is another extrinsic reward; yet increases in pay may give the high achiever a satisfying feeling of successful movement toward goals. In addition, for some employees, so-called extrinsic rewards may carry great value in themselves, or an employee may place great value on a goal for which he sees the particular extrinsic reward as a means. Who would maintain that pay and promotion are not subject to increasingly higher goal aspirations, however we may categorize them as reinforcers? *

* See Cummings and Schwab, *op. cit.,* pp. 34–36, for a discussion of behavior maintenance and a model showing relationships among goal attainment, satisfaction, goal aspiration, and motivation.

2. *Which of the various "small" reinforcers at the organization's disposal (such as approving gestures and minor gifts and privileges) are most likely to produce satiation?*

Study of this issue suggests that the natural social rewards (compliments, attention, recognition) are less likely to produce satiation than "contrived" rewards. Examples of contrived rewards include consumables (coffeebreak treats, free lunches, Easter hams); manipulatables (watches, trophies); visual and auditory rewards (office with a window, piped-in music); and tokens (money, trading stamps, vacation trips).*

The performance of a highly dependent employee may be sustained for a considerable period by the supervisor's repeated expressions of approval. But questions remain: Can natural social reinforcers, even if contingent on performance and comparatively resistant to satiety, sustain performance indefinitely unless other reinforcers are brought into play? Under what conditions will an employee tire of compliments and attention?

3. *Since intrinsic satisfactions appear to be related to the basic nature of the job, can motivation be sustained in an unfitting job?*

The difficulties in such a case are universally recognized. But if heightened levels of aspiration are a factor, is it not possible to find extrinsic reinforcers (social or contrived, large or small) that will raise aspirations among employees in unfitting jobs? Again, are there sources of intrinsic satisfaction in unfitting jobs?

4. *Is individual maturity the answer to sustained motivation — maturity in the sense that an employee is self-reinforcing and controls his own behavior? If so, how do we get there?*

Luthans and Kreitner propose that an employee can be moved toward maturity through positive reinforcement of progressively mature behavior, and that the development of self-control can be aided through (1) participation in goal setting and (2) contingency contracting. They also indicate that self-control is more likely to occur in an "interesting and challenging job" in which the work itself is positively reinforcing than in a tedious job performed or tolerated for contrived reinforcers.†

---

* Luthans and Kreitner, *op. cit.*, pp. 101, 103.
† See Luthans and Kreitner, *op. cit.*, pp. 145–149, for a discussion of the development of maturity and self-control.

The suggested relationship between the nature of the job and maturity raises some practical problems. While an interesting job may be more conducive to mature behavior than a tedious one, the repertoire of jobs within a department is not likely to be wide enough, even under the rare condition of administrative flexibility that permits restructuring of jobs and easy movement of employees between jobs, to provide everyone with a job that is interesting and challenging.

A promising means of sustaining behavior through self-regulation is suggested by Bandura,* who sees reinforcement as regulating behavior through its information-giving and motivational functions and addresses the problem of bringing a person to the point of regulating his own behavior through self-applied reinforcement.

Perhaps the way Bandura suggests is a navigable course. As skill develops, the employee acquires new or modified behaviors; but he should also adopt standards of performance. Incentives and reinforcers, including tangible and external ones, contribute to this process. The coaching supervisor should model behavior and administer rewards in such a way as to teach standards. A reward must be based on achievement and must be clearly connected with the performance it is contingent on. Noncontingent rewards (those not dependent on accomplishment and given indiscriminately for good or poor performance) and rewards related to time on the job rather than to achievement will interfere with the acquisition of standards.

The standards become the basis for the individual's own reinforcement of performance. Apparently, if the standards are developed in a variety of activities, they can become generalized— serving as a level of performance required for self-satisfaction in other activities. Self-regard enters into play to help sustain the performance at or above the standard. Self-esteem and pride are enhanced if the individual performs at that level; they suffer when he falls short of the standard. In addition, self-esteem seems to keep the individual from rewarding himself for substandard performance.

* Bandura, *op. cit.*, pp. 129–139.

What the Operating Manager Can Do

The manager's responsibility does not require him forever to elicit better performance from his subordinates. He must, of course, bring performance to a satisfactory level and hold it there; improving it beyond that point is desirable but may not be practical with all subordinates. The manager may be able to realize the department's economic goals without developing maturity and self-regulated behavior in every employee. But this development must occur in a substantial number of employees if the department is to succeed economically and maintain that success. The manager is left with the problem of determining how to sustain employee performance in a complex mix of people and situations. Some subordinates he will bring along to self-reinforcement and high performance; some he will do less with but still keep at a satisfactory level; some he will be able to do very little with.

In attempting to increase an employee's self-control, the manager may find the job itself to be a basic obstacle. And the assumption that participation in goal setting will aid development may not take into account the numerous indications of the inappropriateness and ineffectiveness of participation. Again, although the connection between the reinforcer and the behavior should be made clear, formal and deliberate contingency contracting has not come forward convincingly as a technique for adults in industrial and commercial operations. Indeed, some managers (and possibly some subordinates) view the contracting arrangement as childlike bargaining and as a reversion to immaturity.

Yet, as noted earlier, there may be practical routes to self-regulated behavior, at least for certain employees. In training the subordinate, is it not possible to inculcate standards of performance that will serve as a basis for self-reinforcement? Is it not possible that such standards of performance will attach to the skill and both endure—even in activities that were not highly prized at the start—at least to the point of making the imposition of external reinforcers or sanctions not an absolute or exclusive requirement indefinitely? And is it not possible for the subordinate to find self-rewards in performance that meets the adopted standards?

Personal satisfaction itself can be a reinforcing consequence of high performance. For the repairman, turning over a finely tuned machine to an operator can be a rewarding experience; for the supervisor, transferring a good departmental operation to the next shift can be reinforcing. Assuming the employee has leeway in scheduling breaks, making his canteen or smoke breaks contingent on having the job in good shape can be a self-reward for good performance. Flexible vacation or leave schedules provide another opportunity for self-reward. Numerous little privileges and treats at the employee's disposal can serve as self-administered rewards for performance. But perhaps the largest self-reward is the personal recognition, through an evaluation against high performance standards, that the performance is good.

As he surveys his workforce, the manager will realize very clearly that self-reinforcement is not the full answer; it is not a realistic objective with all subordinates, although it will be with some. He must look broadly at all factors influencing employee performance and make fitting applications to people and circumstances. A number of these factors are discussed below.

DISTINGUISHING AMONG REWARDS

It is helpful to distinguish between rewards or satisfactions that tend to have a propelling quality and those that simply represent equilibrium, and between rewards that are likely to affect performance in the traditional terms of efficiency and quality and those that may not. Satisfactions such as pay level and promotional opportunities lend themselves to an expansion of goals. Their motivational force will remain strong as long as something further lies ahead and the subordinate increases his level of aspiration as he attains intermediate goals. But in the case of pay level he may stop along the way or push forward, depending on the value of pay to him; if it represents security he may stop earlier than he would if it represented status. Ultimate objectives also affect the renewable motivational strength of promotions. In addition, even if a subordinate raises his promotional sights higher, performance in current job duties may not improve. The subordinate may see the present job as an obstacle calling for patient endurance rather than for increased skill or effort. If promotional possibilities are to serve as a genuine reinforcer of current performance, the contingency must be clearly established.

Such a contingency was not established in the case of Jerome Thompson, who came to the company with his MBA degree and with the expectation that in relatively short order he would be filling an important managerial job. But he realized that he would have to start at the bottom of the ladder and appeared quite happy when he was given a first assignment, after minimum training, as a supervisor in charge of one shift of workers in a section of the Preparation Department.

The department head, Kenneth Ross, stayed close to him and tried to bring him to the point where he could competently handle the full range of supervisory duties. Thompson appeared eager to listen to him and showed quick understanding of what he was told, but his execution of tasks appeared to get worse rather than better.

Efficiency and quality figures for Thompson's section began to drop. This fact came quickly to the attention of the plant manager, Edmund Trent, who called Ross to his office for an explanation. Ross suggested that Thompson's job performance was the major problem. He said that Thompson appeared to lose enthusiasm after he had performed a task, that he seemed to think that once he had "learned" to do it (that is, had done it once or twice), there was no further point in doing it. "His idea of why he's in my department is a lot different from mine," Ross stated.

Social satisfactions appear to reach their more or less fixed potency when a state of social equilibrium is reached. The satisfaction of establishing friendly relationships with a work group is an example. The subordinate is normally concerned with keeping that relationship pleasant rather than with forming or joining groups all over the organization. He may expand his range of acquaintances, but his own work group is usually the compelling social milieu. He needs to be comfortable there. Of course, the balance is not permanent; the subordinate will make renewed efforts when somebody or something tips the scales and brings tension to the relationship. But efforts at social mending are not likely to be aimed at improved job performance as the manager would define it.

The subordinate's relationship with the manager requires

equilibrium as well. In addition to serving as a source of approval and tangible rewards for the subordinate, the manager must appear predictable, approachable, nonthreatening, and "human." The subordinate cannot establish the stable relationship he seeks if the manager is quixotic, unapproachable, or irascible. Once an acceptable relationship is established, the subordinate usually seeks to maintain it rather than to increase the intimacy of the association.

Stability is required in physical job conditions as well as in social relationships. But conditions will directly affect performance. The superior should do what he can, therefore, to make the physical environment safe, comfortable, and pleasant and to maintain such conditions. Lack of stability in job conditions is not only dissatisfying but may trigger other dissatisfactions or become a focus for displaced complaints. Adverse job conditions may be perceived as evidence of lack of personal consideration for employees. Or they may aggravate minor irritations that subordinates normally tolerate and expand into a generalized state of dissatisfaction.

DEALING WITH FITTING AND UNFITTING JOBS

If a job is genuinely appealing to the subordinate and matches his abilities and interests, the intrinsic satisfaction will go far to sustain performance. Is additional reinforcement needed? Sometimes we assume that if an employee really likes his work, additional reinforcement through supervisory recognition and tangible rewards is superfluous. However, the comforting notion that an employee "is happy the way he is" or "doesn't want to be disturbed" is often a delusion. Although skill in a fitting job is indeed intrinsically rewarding, it may not fill all the subordinate's strong needs. He may seek larger goals—through the tangible rewards he feels the skill should command. Underpaying a skilled craftsman, no matter how much he likes his work, will obviously do little for sustaining his motivation.

What about unfitting jobs? Fortunately, certain intrinsic satisfactions are still available to the employee. Experience of success is one such reward—and whatever self-esteem flows from it. Participation in goal setting appears to be another. If the superior stimulates early success and recognizes it, and involves the subordinate in goal setting (with due regard to situation and personality), motivation may improve.

When the job is basically unfitting, the superior must rely much more heavily on extrinsic rewards—tangible and intangible—to sustain the effort. But exclusive or heavy reliance on small, personal gestures is somewhat naive. The small, favorable comments may prove useful in training, to help establish job skills firmly as a matter of habit. Some measure of permanence is thus achieved, but it is a permanence of skills and not necessarily of effort. Eventually, certain employees will be interested in knowing what larger goodies lie behind the cakes and ale and the nod of approval. They will want to know, if they are doing so well, when the next pay raise is due. Sustaining motivation cannot be reduced to such simple terms as the gift of a doughnut or a pat on the back now and then.

It is equally naive to assume that simple gestures (expressions of approval, small tangible rewards) will somehow be translated into increased employee interest in the job—that outside reinforcement will magically endow the job with intrinsic value for the employee. Exposure to and experience in a task may arouse latent interest among some employees, but this is more a matter of uncovering an interest than creating one. And even if performance is sustained by adherence to a general high-level standard, the task itself will not thereby become intrinsically satisfying.

RECOGNIZING INDIVIDUAL DIFFERENCES

After the employee has been trained, his motivation is still a matter of rewards and their significance to him. This brings us again, inevitably, to the decisive role of individual differences.

But there is greater difficulty for the supervisor at this point. During training he could influence (1) the employee's expectation of mastering the job; (2) the actual process of mastering it, using reinforcers as a primary procedure and stimulating early successes; (3) the employee's expectation of rewards contingent on mastering the job; and (4) the realization of the rewards. Now all of this is past. The employee has learned the job, is reaping the related rewards, and is clearly aware of rewards lying ahead. Here the influence of the supervisor diminishes. He will continue to provide what rewards he can and, particularly at times of change, will clarify situations for the employee. But the issue of sustaining effort and remaining on the job is largely up to the employee. His answers to such pertinent questions as these are the compelling ones:

Are there enough rewards?
Is a particular reward satisfying in itself? Does it satisfy a major need?
Is more of the reward wanted?
Does the reward represent a means to higher satisfaction?

The answers will depend on the employee's mixture of motives and on the unique set of characteristics deriving from his temperament, aptitude, experience, and training. The factors of aspiration level, suitability for the job, satiation threshold, and development of maturity are all subject to individual differences.

Consider, for example, the case of Robert Edwards. It has been a trying but good year for him. In February he was promoted to the position of superintendent of warehousing and shipping and improved the operation month by month. Early in the game he revised the carton identification system to expedite the retrieval of stored merchandise and the loading of carriers. Things were in a mess for a time, but he had the active support of his superior, Claude Hinson, the plant manager; and he persisted in his effort until the system began to pay off. Later in the year he turned his attention to employee performance. Again, the results were favorable: individual efficiency went up and labor costs went down. Again, Hinson was strongly supportive.

Indeed, Hinson's coaching efforts were masterful. He intruded neither too much nor too little, gradually bringing Edwards to an independent execution of responsibilities. He expressed approval not only of objective results but of what he judged (accurately, as it turned out) to be effective activities.

When the year-end salary reviews were completed, Hinson announced to Edwards that he had been granted an increase of eight percent. Edwards did not respond very enthusiastically. Two weeks later Edwards informed Hinson that he was leaving the company for another job. He explained, "I am not a fool. I know—you told me so a hundred times—that I did a good job. I really turned a pretty lousy operation around. So what happened? I get an eight percent raise, and everybody and his brother got at least seven percent, no matter what kind of job they did. Not only that, but I understand that the seven percent was intended mainly to offset the increase in living cost—and to enable us to keep pace with the hourly paid employees who were raised seven percent earlier in the year. So what my eight percent boils down to is a measly one percent for merit. One lousy percent for all that effort and all that accomplishment, as you yourself called it. Many times. Well, if all I get for it is a lot of words and a lousy one percent, the devil with it!"

FINDING GUIDANCE IN THE MAZE

A review of the complex problem of sustaining performance may bring the manager to the discouraging conclusion that very little can be done. If he begins his review with an exaggerated idea of his control, he may despair at the end of exercising any control at all. Yet his experience informs him that he is not helpless. The wise course is to replace naive optimism with measured optimism based on a realistic view of the difficulties and the use of insightful actions. The manager's efforts may be enhanced if he has a clear sense of the intricate interplay between reinforcer and employee. Table 7 is an outline which, at the risk of oversimplification, presents various kinds of reinforcers and conditions under which they might serve to sustain performance.

How Much Motivation Is Required?

While we should not deprecate the importance of motivation, it is useful—and sometimes consoling—to realize that strong motivation may not have a totally favorable influence on job performance and that a decrease in motivation may not have an intolerably unfavorable influence. We know, for example, that extremely strong motivation can lead to difficulties in learning; the subordinate may become impatient with the step-by-step progression required for genuine development of skill. The employee may be so occupied

TABLE 7.
Reinforcers and possible sustaining conditions.

Reinforcer	Conditions
Extrinsic rewards	
Natural social rewards	If employee is not overly concerned
Praise and approval	with higher rewards
Information on good perfor-	If employee is dependent
mance	If employee is in training status
Recognition	
Contrived rewards	If employee is not overly concerned
Tokens	with higher rewards
Edibles	If satiety does not occur
Gifts	
Privileges	
Pay and promotion	If aspiration level increases
	If it is a means to higher life goals
Intrinsic rewards	
Fitting job	If employee does not also view it as worthy of higher extrinsic rewards that he is not receiving, or as a means to larger life satisfactions that are not being fulfilled
Experience of success	If employee is in a fitting job; likely to work only temporarily in an unfitting job, but effect may be somewhat prolonged if a high level of skill is acquired and efficacy expectations are enhanced
Participation	If appropriate to personality and situation; if consistently contingent on good performance
Self-satisfaction	If firmly attached to standards of performance

with getting there that he neglects the necessary means. A related problem is the direction strong motivation takes, since job performance is a complex combination of task execution, results, priorities, and emphases. If the motivation stirs effort powerfully in one direction, certain aspects of the job may be handled minimally or avoided, and the total performance may be thrown out of balance. A strong drive for output and related earnings, for example, may have a stultifying effect on maintenance of product quality and employee safety. Such imbalance occurs frequently in the performance of experienced employees. The superior's task, then, is to ensure not so much that the motivation is extremely strong as that it is adequate for job learning and for the achievement of job objectives.

Loss of motivation must be considered in relation to overall job performance as well as to specific aspects of performance. To a certain degree, high-level skill tends to become autonomous, to be expressed somewhat independently of (or at least not so obviously in association with) fluctuations in the employee's motivational state. Habits take strong hold. Moreover, if lessened motivation is indeed reflected in the performance of the highly skilled employee, the performance level may still remain high enough to meet normal requirements of the job. If the employee is exceptionally skilled and efficient, performance may be acceptable even with a slackening of effort. The effort may have a sufficient payoff in the total job.

Finally, motivational loss may affect various aspects of the job differently. But if major job objectives are upheld we can sometimes tolerate lesser performance in other aspects. With a truly competent subordinate in a complex or demanding job, output will probably be affected more than quality or professionalism of performance. The employee is likely to do less than he can, but what he does he will still do well. A real professional, with high standards firmly underlying his performance, will be hard put to botch up an assignment.

If these conclusions are correct—and experience seems to support them—they argue for quick and strong development of job skill and performance standards so that, even when the employee's motivation and effort diminish, he will continue to fulfill the major criteria of job performance.

As we have seen, reinforcers are useful to such early and strong development, even in jobs found eventually to be uninteresting or insufficiently rewarding. Skills tend to develop under positive reinforcement, and the development itself is usually intrinsically rewarding. Reinforcers which have helped to mold the skill may be inadequate to sustain the employee's later efforts. But even if the manager is unable to nurture the employee's skill to its full expression, if he has done a good job of training the employee may settle into an acceptable level of performance. If the manager reaches this modest position with his subordinates, perhaps he has done as much as he can within the practical limits of his position and the uncertain state of the art.

Continuing the Effort

The search goes on for a means of ensuring continued motivation and continued high-level performance. We have examined motivation primarily in regard to its favorable influence on job performance, which in turn has a favorable influence on company objectives—primarily productivity. Yet as every manager knows—and as we have seen all along the way—employee motivation is not always expressed through improved job performance; some employee satisfactions may be realized through other outcomes. A basic issue, therefore, is the possibility of meeting both objectives: productivity and employee satisfaction. Research continues in the matter, along with an attempt to read meaning into the findings from earlier research.

A multidisciplinary group, supported by a grant to New York University from the National Science Foundation, conducted a revealing evaluation of the research on factors affecting productivity and job satisfaction. The evaluation produced a list of ingredients considered critical to attaining these two objectives:

a. Financial compensation of workers must be linked to their performance and to productivity gains.
b. Workers and work must be matched so as to create a work situation which workers will see as capable of meeting their needs and expectations, and where they will have the capabilities and resources to be successful.
c. For workers who desire it, their work should provide opportunity for full use of their abilities, making a meaningful contribution, having challenging and diversified duties, and being responsible for others.

    d. Workers at all levels must have inputs to plans and decisions affecting their jobs and working lives.

    e. Appropriate resources, including work methods and equipment, must be provided to facilitate workers' performance and minimize obstacles to carrying out their jobs.

    f. Adequate "hygiene" conditions must exist, including competent and considerate supervision, fair pay and fringe benefits, job security, good working conditions, and sound employee relations.*

While the reviewers recognize that research is not conclusive on these points (we have taken note of swampy research footing in this and the preceding chapter), they see progress toward the dual objectives as unlikely if most of the ingredients are absent. In their view, the principle of critical mass is compelling. That is, the scales are not likely to be tipped significantly in favor of improved productivity and satisfaction unless the effort is "deep and far reaching," to the extent of changing the sociotechnical system.†

The harried operating manager, faced repeatedly with the choice of accepting or rejecting the current panacea, will heartily endorse the idea that a broad effort is required. Unfortunately, he is not in a position to tip the scales, since he controls only a part of the critical mass. And he must be excused, or at least understood, if he becomes somewhat skeptical of certain means being urged on him, within his limited jurisdiction, to achieve results. He may feel, for example, that recommendations from some social scientists are primarily expressions of an article of faith: that the open, participative style of managing is superior, both morally and practically, and will bring productivity to the organization and satisfaction to its employees. If the manager accepts such recommendations and attempts to put them into practice, he may find himself in a rather awkward position. If he succeeds with the participative style, the belief of the advocates is confirmed. If he fails, the result can be interpreted as a failure of execution. The basic dogma is intact. The manager may conclude that his mission is not to find out if participation will work for him—that's a given—but to make it work.

* Raymond A. Katzell, Daniel Yankelovich, et al., *Productivity and Job Satisfaction* (New York: The Psychological Corporation, 1975), pp. 38–39.

† Katzell, Yankelovich, et al., *op. cit.,* pp. 24–25.

Of course, in a number of cases, participation has indeed been found to be related positively to satisfaction and to implementation of decisions. But the less restrained advocates, apparently believing that the participative approach is consistent with a true reading of employee behavior, may tend to push beyond an explicit reading of the findings. Is not the truth the truth? Thus they may move from research to loosely supported speculation—and, further, to a somewhat dogmatic prescription for leadership behavior in industry.

There is little doubt that personal values and beliefs seep into the interpretation of behavioral research findings. Lorsch's recommendations in this matter are refreshing and highly pertinent. To help us judge the work of others more objectively, he suggests asking these questions: What is the author trying to accomplish? What are his/her values? What is his/her intellectual heritage? What concepts and variables does the author use? Are they clearly defined? What data does the study provide? What are the limits of generalizing from that data to other situations? If the author makes prescriptions, to what extent are they consistent with the author's personal values? * Lorsch advises those who do research and write to state explicitly their cultural heritage, values, and view of human motivation; to be explicit about the situational conditions under which data are collected; and to define explicitly their concepts and variables.

* Jay W. Lorsch, "Managers, Behavioral Scientists, and the Tower of Babel," in Cass and Zimmer, *op. cit.*, p. 254.

CHAPTER 8

Making Training
Pertinent

T HE IDEA that training and experience are not necessarily the good and true means of maintaining effective performance may appear somewhat heretical. Yet any manager with eyesight has observed well-trained and highly successful supervisors who proved dismal blunderers when they were imported or transferred into a new assignment, and initially successful supervisors whose performance degenerated in an unchanging assignment as their training and experience increased.

The Situational Factor in Leadership

Fiedler and Chemers have thrown light on this phenomenon for puzzled executives by emphasizing the importance of the situation in leadership effectiveness and by indicating that the fit of supervisory style and situation may be upset as the manager gains experience and receives training.*

It has long been realized that training programs are not appro-

* Fiedler and Chemers, *op. cit.*

priate in all situations and with all subordinates. Nevertheless, we tend to accept certain training topics as universally useful to performance, no matter who the supervisor is or what the nature of his situation might be. The more gullible among us may endow a large number of such programs with catholic virtues—and there are certainly enough programs around to exhaust our blessings: sensitivity training, MBO and its various spinoffs, organizational development, transactional analysis (in the plant, the office, the church, the home, the nursery, or wherever two or three are gathered together), job enrichment, the managerial grid, behavior modification, contingency contracting, role negotiation, assertiveness training. The list goes on. Whatever appears under the guise of behavioral science is likely to be pressed on managerial and supervisory personnel as good for them and as the way to operate. The potential for frustration in such uncritical acceptance of programs is great. Hence, the superior's plaint: "If it's so good for them, why don't they use it?" Or, if they use it, "Why doesn't it work?"

Stogdill's summary of the relationship found in research studies between various patterns of leadership behavior and three criteria of effectiveness (productivity, follower satisfaction, and group cohesiveness) is revealing. Only one leadership pattern contributes positively to all the criteria: "structuring expectations." As Stogdill expresses it: "This pattern of behavior is perhaps the central factor in leadership, since it is intimately associated with the definition of leadership as the initiation and maintenance of structure in expectation and interaction. Philosophies of leadership and training methods that undermine this factor destroy the very foundation of leadership." * Person-oriented behaviors are not consistently related to productivity, but they are related to follower satisfaction; participation and considerate behaviors are also related to group cohesiveness.

For operating managers, productivity is the essential criterion. And while it may be comforting to know that employees are satisfied and groups cohesive, these objectives tend to be sec-

---

* Stogdill, *op. cit.,* p. 419.

ondary. Indeed, they may be primarily valued for the degree to which they are seen as contributing to productivity. But that contribution, as managers know from experience, may be neither large nor reliable. Operating managers have often noted that a highly satisfied employee is not necessarily a highly productive one.

The flaw in many behavioral science approaches, from the manager's point of view, is that they stress democratic and participative procedures—the very leadership behaviors that are questionable means of increasing productivity. The industrial trainer with a limited budget must make a choice among programs for the supervisor. While the trainer may recognize the differences in effect between structuring and other work-centered approaches (and the difficulty of making practical distinctions among them) and regard job satisfaction as a worthy objective, he may conclude that the supervisor's best interests are served by giving him training that is largely structuring, or related to structuring, in purpose and nature. Thus training in the technology of the operation would appear to be highly useful. Equally valuable is training in the policies, procedures, operating practices, systems, and controls that govern the handling of common job and employee-relations problems and provide some measure of progress. A viable organization does not leave policies and procedures to the improvisation of individual managers and supervisors, or to be used or not used at their discretion.

It is in the execution of these policies and procedures and in the gray area of administration where programmed solutions do not fit that further crucial decisions about training must be made. Ample room exists here for further structuring, for participative styles, or whatever. Do we train the supervisor to play it loosely or tightly or somewhere in between? Or do we shift from one style to another?

Selecting the "Right" Kind of Training

If training should be selective, how do we make the right choices of topics and programs beyond the start, as the supervisor gains experience? Fiedler and Chemers propose that we use training to "teach the leader how to modify leadership situations so that they match his personality." * Whether training in any traditional sense or training within the competence of line management would serve this function is doubtful. Beyond giving the leader insight into the correspondence between motivational pattern and situation, what can we do through training? Fiedler talks about increasing or decreasing position power and changing the structure of the task—that is, influencing two of the elements in his definition of the situation—to permit the manager to behave in his characteristic way, whether employee-oriented or task-oriented.

Certainly basic questions on the objectives and efficacy of training must be resolved with reference to leadership style and situation. If a manager's style is ineffective in a rather inflexible situation, can we modify his behavior, against the grain of his primary motivation, in an effort to make him perform more effectively? And if a situation compatible with his natural style changes, can we help him make the necessary adjustments in behavior? Vroom apparently sees more flexibility in leadership behavior and more potential for modifying leadership style through training and development than does Fiedler.†

It is widely held that leadership style can be changed, despite its roots in temperament and motivation, and that a subordinate can be taught to adapt to situational demands even though he is "uncomfortable" in doing so. Some pliability must exist; otherwise, organizations would be hard put to function at all. Points at issue here are the extent to which behavior can be changed and the durability of the change. Obviously, rapid or frequent shifting would place a heavy demand on the individual's adaptability and intelligence; and if these are limited, the response may be minimal. In addition, evidence suggests that the leader tends to return to his characteristic pattern of behavior when the going gets rough and the situation becomes stressful.

It has been suggested recently in the literature that changes in temperament and motivation (the achievement motive as the favor-

---

* Fiedler and Chemers, op. cit., p. 148.
† Victor H. Vroom, "Leadership Revisited," in Cass and Zimmer, op. cit., p. 234.

ite example) can be wrought through training. While it would be absurd to argue against the developmental nature of these characteristics—they are certainly environmentally produced—we must question whether significant changes can be effected at this late date, when the adult employee comes on the scene as a subordinate.

In the face of all the uncertainties, limitations, and cautions, what can we advise the operating superior to do? It is the responsibility of the trainer to draw the long bow and make definite recommendations—not with the assurance that they will always work but with the expectation that the probabilities will be favorable if they are tried. The recommendations might include the following:

1. Accept the thesis that the situation is a major factor in leadership effectiveness, and that the happiest case is one where the leader's natural style (based on temperament and motivation) is compatible with the demands of the situation. Thus, when a department or operation requires organization, the task-oriented individual will fit best. When cultivation of relationships is the chief requirement, the employee-oriented individual will fit best.

2. Attempt to place the subordinate initially in a job where his natural style is likely to be effective. Such placement requires an expansion of the usual selection or promotion procedure to identify the subordinate's natural style and the types of situations in which he has been especially effective or ineffective.

3. Take the position that, in a manufacturing enterprise, there are certain structuring skills which all subordinates must develop and which are pertinent in any situation. These skills should be emphasized in the early stages of the subordinate's training.

4. Take the position that the temperament or motivation of the subordinate cannot be changed but that most subordinates can change their supervisory behavior to some extent to meet the situation. The superior should be alert to changes in the subordinate's situation that call for an adjustment in leadership style and should train the subordinate in skillful execution of the new behaviors. But he should also prepare the subordinate, insofar as clear and practical models are available, to detect signs of situational changes and

to determine the style modifications indicated—with the realistic expectation that the subordinate's perceptions of changes in the situation will not become extremely sensitive nor his responses extremely subtle or optimally adaptable.

5. Accept the probability that some subordinates will not be able to adapt their leadership style sufficiently to be effective. Such individuals should be transferred to a more fitting assignment.

We are now ready to examine how certain of these factors come prominently into play in training the new supervisor.

Dealing with the New Supervisor

In preparing the new supervisor for managing an assignment, it is advisable to begin by teaching him the task-oriented aspects, the technology and procedures, and to emphasize those behaviors that are likely to have a favorable effect on productivity but, at the same time, are not likely to have an unfavorable impact on employee satisfaction. The new supervisor cannot afford to let production drop while he adjusts to the job, and he must begin by laying the basis for a sound relationship with employees. Fortunately, research points to the possibility of favorable effects in regard to both objectives through a structuring approach—specifically, the structuring of employee expectations, or letting employees know what to expect. By keeping roles straight and structuring expectations, the new supervisor can prevent productivity from deteriorating to the point where drastic task-centered measures are needed and may establish a solid basis for building salutary working relationships later on. His first order of business is to organize his job, but in such a way as to avoid an abrasive effect on relationships.

The new supervisor should be made aware that the effectiveness of his behavior is significantly dependent on the situation. As he moves further into the assignment, we must help him diagnose his changing situation, adjust his behaviors accordingly, and execute them competently. But how do we go about preparing the supervisor to size up the situation and determine pertinent behaviors?

Fortunately, some guidance is emerging in the literature. Fiedler and his collaborators provide a formula for measuring the situational variables of position power, task structure, and leader–member relations as a basis for identifying appropriate kinds of behavior—whether task-oriented or employee-oriented.* Reddin gives a framework for analyzing the situation in terms of technology demands and human element and organizational demands and for settling on appropriate kinds of behavior.† Hersey and Blanchard relate the amount of task behavior or relationship behavior a leader should provide to the level of functioning—from immature to mature—of the leader's followers.‡ Other situational factors that might be considered in determining appropriate leadership style are time demands and the running condition of the operation.

In spite of the emerging models, situational analysis is not an established art. Defining the situation is still a problem; even though there is considerable overlap, the variables differ from model to model. Further, the diagnosis is probably too complex for the average supervisor to master. And the leap from the defined situation to the fitting supervisory behavior is an uncertain venture. Research on this point has considerable distance to go.

Still, assuming we can make a valid prescription of behaviors, can the supervisor manage them? If more structuring is required, such as a stricter designation of job methods and a closer follow-up on performance, the supervisor is in position to provide it. But how well? There are degrees of skill even in carrying out such straightforward activities, and poor execution of appropriate behaviors may be as disastrous as reliance on inappropriate behaviors. If the situation correctly calls for employee-centered behaviors, execution becomes even more troublesome. It is difficult enough to transmit information to employees and explain supervisory actions adequately. But how does a supervisor execute "participation"?

---

* Fred E. Fiedler, Martin M. Chemers, and Linda Mahar, *Improving Leadership Effectiveness* (New York: John Wiley & Sons, 1976).

† William J. Reddin, *Managerial Effectiveness* (New York: McGraw-Hill Book Company, 1970).

‡ See Robert H. Guest, Paul Hersey, and Kenneth H. Blanchard, *Organizational Change through Effective Leadership* (Englewood Cliffs, N.J.: Prentice-Hall, 1977), pp. 19–20, for a short statement of the four different maturity levels requiring different leadership styles according to the Hersey-Blanchard situational leadership theory.

What distinguishes good execution from poor? Genuine from ersatz? The backfiring possibilities from poor efforts to provide participation are great; yet we are ill equipped as trainers to instruct
the supervisor in its use—to define participation and translate it
into activities, and to guide him in the execution. The point is that
our task is not complete when we designate the pertinent behaviors; skillful execution must follow, and we must train the
supervisor for such execution, despite the difficulties.

At this stage of our knowledge, it is unrealistic to expect supervisors to change their situations substantially to match their natural
leadership style—or to expect trainers to provide much help in
such an undertaking. A more practical approach to maintaining
effective performance is to change behaviors with the situation,
despite the difficulties and training problems involved, especially in
teaching employee-centered activities.

The fundamental question, then, is whether we can rely on
supervisors to make the behavioral adaptations that ever changing
situations seem to demand. There is no absolute assurance. Yet
experience suggests that most supervisors are at least moderately
adaptable, that they can change behaviors if they are helped to do
so. Those who find it impossible to adjust because of rigid temperament, motivation, and habits are necessarily limited in the job
situations they can fill—if any can be found. The most rigid among
them may be unsuitable for supervisory work altogether, since no
production department remains stable indefinitely, and the basic
continuity of the operation does not allow for constant shifting of
supervisory personnel.

Supervisory Behavior and Situational Change

What behaviors do industrial supervisors customarily exhibit? I
made a careful analysis of behaviors found to be typical of "good"
first-line supervisors (shift foremen), classifying the behaviors as
task-oriented (primarily structuring) or employee-oriented.
Employee-oriented behaviors were further grouped under the sub-
headings of concern, information, and participation. Here are the
results, in terms of numbers of behaviors in each category:

		Employee-Oriented Behaviors			
		Use of Information			
Task-Oriented Behaviors	Expression of Concern	Feedback	Information (Down)	Response to Information (Up)	Participation
38	6	2	7	4	1

Although the items were not clear-cut and the classification is arguable, the general conclusion would appear indisputable:

1. Effective shift foremen are, in large part, task-oriented. Moreover, a considerable percentage of employee-focused behaviors are clearly structuring in purpose. They tell the employee what is expected of him.

2. Most employee-centered activities are concerned with giving information. Participation is virtually absent; it appears only in safety matters. The more effective supervisors tend to express concern for employees and to give information, but they do not permit any significant amount of participation. They respond readily to employees' questions but apparently do not usually invite questions from employees and certainly do not invite solutions from them.

If these findings are typical,* the representative industrial supervisor engages primarily in structuring activities and does not shift very much to employee-centered behaviors, whatever the situation. It is possible that he would do better if he engaged more heavily in employee-centered behaviors, but he has not found this out. Considering the nature of industrial supervisory jobs and the criteria by which supervisory performance is judged, structuring is the indicated way to go. The supervisor is no fool. Structuring has a demonstrably favorable effect on production, for which the supervisor is held accountable, and there is usually no comparable emphasis on employee satisfaction or comparable index for measurement. Turnover, absenteeism, and grievance rate are only indirect indications of employee satisfaction, and the typical operating manager will tolerate a relatively poor showing in these

* One must be wary, of course, of generalizing. Less direct knowledge of supervisors in other companies at least suggests to me that the pattern of behavior I describe is widespread.

measures—as long as departmental output or efficiency is not significantly affected.

We may wonder whether the major criterion of operating effectiveness—productivity—will permit a much greater emphasis on employee-centered activities unless there is more convincing evidence that such behaviors will increase production. It is unlikely that the productivity criterion will be displaced, and little reason that it should be.

While we can seriously doubt that employee-centered behaviors by the supervisor are a wise way to go about increasing employee productivity, these behaviors can bring rewards and satisfactions that, in certain circumstances and with certain employees, are effective in sustaining and improving job performance. We have examined the conditions under which such results might occur. The supervisors' argument is not against employee satisfaction as a legitimate objective, but supervisors cannot regard it as their exclusive or primary objective. They will not fail to see that some employees respond to their employee-oriented behaviors with increased effort. But they do not accept this approach as the chief route to productivity. The supervisor would be happy to find a practical way to bring about both productivity and a satisfied workforce. A far-reaching effort is required, as discussed.

What limited effect a supervisor can have in this effort may depend largely on his ability to adapt his behavior to the situation and to the individual as part of it. A company is well advised to consider the relationship between supervisory behavior and the situation. Guided by certain gross situational signs, even if diagnosis is rather imprecise, the company should move supervisors into heavier use of relationship activities when indicated and prepare supervisors for the need to make at least limited adaptations.

For example, there is little doubt that a department in very poor operating condition requires structuring by the supervisor to get it off the ground. And when things are running reasonably well, it is advisable to shore up relationships with employees. Up to this point, experience seems to support Fiedler's findings that task-oriented behaviors are appropriate in unfavorable situations and employee-oriented behaviors appropriate when the situation is moderately favorable for the supervisor. A further indication in Fiedler's study, that structuring is appropriate when the situation is highly favorable, would seem to fly in the face of experience unless—and this may be the key—the structuring takes a different form.

In a highly unfavorable situation, the pertinent task-centered behaviors are likely to be direct orders and close surveillance to ensure that everything and everyone are in place and functioning as required. In highly favorable circumstances, the supervisor's chief task may be to maintain good operating conditions—a structuring activity to some extent—by providing employees with the wherewithal to do the job (supplies, materials, support services) and keeping a close watch on this but otherwise moving out of the way.

Certainly the approach should take into account the type of job held by the employee, his level of skill, and the sort of person he is. Ultimately these considerations lead to a recognition of individual differences—a concept that most good supervisors live by. As a rather obvious example, the supervisor is likely to permit more independence of action in a highly skilled repairman with years of experience on the job than in a new employee in a less skilled job. The supervisor does not have to tell the trained repairman what to do and when to do it. This tendency to allow independence of action is likely to be stronger if the experienced employee has a history of responsible performance and conduct, demonstrating true maturity, and has displayed interest in the company's welfare as well as his own. In such a case, very little attention appears to be required, and conditions are propitious for participation, for consulting with the employee on job-related matters and perhaps on technical matters of wider scope.

This much pliability would seem to be within the capacity of most supervisors: to structure matters more when the operation is running very poorly; to avoid neglecting relationships when things improve; to be structuring with new employees; and to allow independence to mature employees, especially those in highly skilled jobs.

When conditions are conducive to an increase in employee-centered activities, the supervisor may (1) give employees information for purposes other than structuring (giving information not only on his decisions but on the reasons behind them, for example) and (2) provide opportunities for employee participation. As suggested earlier, participation is an open field, rarely used, and virtually unexplored by supervisors.

Drastic and abrupt shifts in style are likely to prove self-defeating. Fortunately, in the normal course of events, the situation in an operating department changes gradually and in relatively small degree. Within this framework, the supervisor can adjust his behaviors to the evolving situation. These shifts need not be radical or dramatic. Thus the supervisor avoids giving the impression of being capricious or quixotic.

As suggested, early in his training the new supervisor needs the knowledge and skills to structure his operation. Even communication with employees in the recommended interview training is largely structuring. In the early course on motivation, the new supervisor should be given an understanding of the motivational effect of employee-centered behaviors. And he should be made aware of how situational changes relate to leadership effectiveness—at least to the extent of understanding the need for adapting his behavior. It is too early in training, however, to burden the supervisor with instruction in diagnosing situations and identifying appropriate behaviors.

This is not to deny that the supervisor needs skill in analyzing situations and executing employee-centered behaviors if the diagnosis points to them. But the diagnosis realistically cannot be complex, and the shift in behaviors need not be—indeed, cannot be—extreme. The time for developing such skills is after the basic structuring of the job has been mastered. Coaching is the indicated technique for such training, although insights can also be given in class and by consultation. We must recognize, however, that no coach can serve as a complete model, since each supervisor is a unique part of the situation he is in.

This is not to suggest that, because the supervisor does influence the situation, he can change it at his will to fit his "natural" supervisory style. If a supervisor is uncomfortable in his environment and stays in it, he is likely to make an effort to modify it. But the degree to which a first-line supervisor can affect the total situation, considering all aspects, is decidedly limited. The supervisory job is circumscribed by a formidable set of policies, procedures, practices, union contract clauses, and controls (in the form of a reporting system for operational results). These constraints direct and delimit the supervisor's actions and, to some extent, measure their effect. (We teach him to manage by such procedures and provisions.) There is, to be sure, some leeway in administration. The supervisor does have space, though restricted, to maneuver within this framework; he can be a strict or loose constructionist. But he cannot ignore the framework or dismantle it or significantly add to it or modify it.

Of course, we must question whether, if the supervisor really had the privilege of clearing the way for exercising his natural style, the effectiveness of the operation would thus be ensured. The resulting fit, in terms of desired company objectives, may be wrong. But, as a practical matter, no company can permit its supervisors an unrestrained hand to "engineer" situations.

The way to go, we can reasonably conclude, is to prepare supervisors as best we can to adjust their behaviors, within a modest range, to fit the usually slowly changing situation.

Bibliography

Atkinson, John W., and Norman T. Feathers, eds. *A Theory of Achievement Motivation.* New York: John Wiley & Sons, 1966.

Bandura, Albert. *Social Learning Theory.* Englewood Cliffs, N.J.: Prentice-Hall, 1977.

Campbell, John P., et al. *Managerial Behavior, Performance, and Effectiveness.* New York: McGraw-Hill Book Company, 1970.

Carroll, Stephen J., Jr., and Henry L. Tosi, Jr. *Management by Objectives: Applications and Research.* New York: Macmillan Publishing Company, 1973.

Cass, Eugene L., and Frederick G. Zimmer, eds. *Man and Work in Society.* New York: Van Nostrand Reinhold Company, 1975.

Connellan, Thomas K. *How to Improve Human Performance: Behaviorism in Business and Industry.* New York: Harper & Row, 1978.

Cummings, L. L., and Donald P. Schwab. *Performance in Organizations: Determinants and Appraisal.* Glenview, Ill.: Scott, Foresman and Company, 1973.

Fiedler, Fred E., and Martin M. Chemers. *Leadership and Effective Management.* Glenview Ill.: Scott, Foresman and Company, 1974.

Fiedler, Fred E., Martin M. Chemers, and Linda Mahar. *Improving Leadership Effectiveness.* New York: John Wiley & Sons, 1976.

Gardner, James E. *Helping Employees Develop Job Skill: A Casebook of Training Approaches.* Washington, D.C.: The Bureau of National Affairs, 1976.

Gardner, James E. *Safety Training for the Supervisor.* Reading, Mass.: Addison-Wesley Publishing Company, 1969. (2nd ed., 1979.)

Guest, Robert H., Paul Hersey, and Kenneth H. Blanchard. *Organizational Change Through Effective Leadership.* Englewood Cliffs, N.J.: Prentice-Hall, 1977.

Harless, J. H. *An Ounce of Analysis (Is Worth a Pound of Objectives).* McLean, Va.: Harless Performance Guild, 1975.

Hersey, Paul, and Kenneth H. Blanchard. *Management of Organizational Behavior: Utilizing Human Resources.* Englewood Cliffs, N.J.: Prentice-Hall, 1969.

Katzell, Raymond A., Daniel Yankelovich, et al. *Work, Productivity, and Job Satisfaction.* New York: The Psychological Association, 1975.

Kepner, Charles H., and Benjamin B. Tregoe. *The Rational Manager.* New York: McGraw-Hill Book Company, 1965.

Laird, Dugan, and Richard Grote. *Solving Management Problems.* Reading, Mass.: Addison-Wesley Publishing Company, 1971.

Lee, Irving J., ed. *Customs and Crises in Communication.* New York: Harper & Brothers, 1954.

Lee, Irving J., and Laura L. Lee. *Handling Barriers in Communication.* New York: Harper & Brothers, 1957.

Lorsch, Jay W. "Managers, Behavioral Scientists, and the Tower of Babel," in Eugene L. Cass and Frederick G. Zimmer, eds., *Man and Work in Society.* New York: Van Nostrand Reinhold Company, 1975, pp. 246–255.

Luthans, Fred, and Robert Kreitner. *Organizational Behavior Modification.* Glenview, Ill.: Scott, Foresman and Company, 1975.

Mager, Robert F., and Peter Pipe. *Analyzing Performance, or "You Really Oughta Wanna."* Belmont, Cal.: Fearon Publishers, 1970.

McClelland, David C., and Robert S. Steele, eds. *Human Motivation: A Book of Readings.* Morristown, N.J.: General Learning Press, 1973.

McGehee, William, and Paul W. Thayer. *Training in Business and Industry.* New York: John Wiley & Sons, 1961.

Porter, Lyman W., and Richard M. Steers. "Organizational, Work, and Personal Factors in Employee Turnover and Absenteeism." *Psychological Bulletin,* Vol. 80, No. 2 (1973), pp. 151–176.

Raia, Anthony P. *Managing by Objectives.* Glenview, Ill.: Scott, Foresman and Company, 1974.

Reddin, William J. *Managerial Effectiveness.* New York: McGraw-Hill Book Company, 1970.

Stogdill, Ralph M. *Handbook of Leadership: A Survey of Theory and Research.* New York: The Free Press, 1974.

Trotta, Maurice S. *Handling Grievances: A Guide for Management and Labor.* Washington, D.C.: The Bureau of National Affairs, 1976.

Trotta, Maurice S. *Supervisor's Handbook on Insubordination.* Washington, D.C.: The Bureau of National Affairs, 1967.

Vaill, Peter. "Understanding High-Performance Systems." Audio cassette tape of presentation at 1978 Conference of the American Society for Training and Development. Madison, Wisc.: ASTD, 1978.

Vroom, Victor H. "Leadership Revisited," in Eugene L. Cass, Frederick G. Zimmer, eds., *Man and Work in Society.* New York: Van Nostrand Reinhold Company, 1975, pp. 220–234.

Vroom, Victor H., and Philip W. Yetton. *Leadership and Decision Making.* Pittsburgh: University of Pittsburgh Press, 1973.

Yoder, Dale, and Herbert G. Heneman, Jr., eds. *ASPA Handbook of Personnel and Industrial Relations. Vol. 5, Training and Development.* Washington, D.C.: The Bureau of National Affairs, 1977.

Index